The Message of Jesus: Large Print

The Message of Jesus

Words That Changed the World

978-1-7910-3421-4 *Paperback*
978-1-7910-3422-1 *eBook*
978-1-7910-3426-9 *Large Print*

DVD
978-1-7910-3425-2

Leader Guide
978-1-7910-3423-8
978-1-7910-3424-5 *eBook*

Also by Adam Hamilton

24 Hours That Changed the World

Christianity and World Religions

Christianity's Family Tree

Confronting the Controversies

Creed

Enough

Faithful

Final Words from the Cross

Forgiveness

Half Truths

Incarnation

John

Leading Beyond the Walls

Living Unafraid

Love to Stay

Luke

Making Sense of the Bible

Moses

Not a Silent Night

Prepare the Way for the Lord

Revival

Seeing Gray in a World of Black and White

Simon Peter

Speaking Well

The Call

The Journey

The Lord's Prayer

The Walk

The Way

Unafraid

When Christians Get It Wrong

Wrestling with Doubt, Finding Faith

Words of Life

Why?

For more information, visit AdamHamilton.com.

ADAM HAMILTON

Author of *John, The Walk,* and *24 Hours That Changed the World*

THE MESSAGE OF JESUS

WORDS THAT CHANGED THE WORLD

LARGE PRINT

Abingdon Press | Nashville

The Message of Jesus
Words That Changed the World
Large Print

Original hardcover edition can be found under
Library of Congress Control Number: 2024944639
978-1-7910-3426-9

MANUFACTURED IN THE UNITED STATES OF AMERICA

To Susan Salley

With gratitude for her partnership and encouragement in the ministry of writing and publishing.
I will be forever grateful.

Contents

Introduction

Within Christianity there has always been a strong emphasis on Christ's death and resurrection. When Paul summarized the gospel that he preached among the Corinthians he noted, "I passed on to you as most important what I also received: Christ died for our sins in line with the scriptures, he was buried, and he rose on the third day in line with the scriptures." (1 Corinthians 15:3-4).

Paul hardly mentions Jesus's words in his letters. In fact, throughout the thirteen letters attributed to Paul in the New Testament, Paul alludes to things consistent with what Jesus said, but only directly quotes Jesus once, in 1 Corinthians 11:23-25, where Paul records Jesus's words at the Last Supper.[1] The same is true in the remaining eight New Testament epistles. Nor do the creeds of the early church, the Apostles' Creed, the Nicene Creed and the Chalcedonian Creed, quote Jesus's teachings.

It is little surprise, therefore, that when Christians today summarize their faith, they often do so by speaking of Jesus's death for their sins and his resurrection.

Yet the four New Testament Gospels record over forty thousand words that Jesus spoke. Accounting for duplicates, where the same saying appears in more than one Gospel, we have approximately twenty-five thousand unique words of Jesus.

And while Matthew, Mark, Luke, and John, the New Testament Gospels, emphasize the Crucifixion and Resurrection as the climax of Jesus's life and ministry, they clearly believed Jesus's words mattered. Simon Peter said of Jesus's teaching, "You have the words of eternal life" (John 6:68).

The words of eternal life. His words were consequential. If you want to follow Jesus today, it is not enough to know that he died and rose again. You are meant to know what he taught about God and God's will for humanity. We're meant not only to embrace these words, but to seek to live them.

In this book, I've captured some of the most important words of Jesus from all four of the Gospels. In the pages that follow, we'll start by seeking to understand the central focus of Jesus's preaching in Matthew, Mark, and Luke: the kingdom of God. Then we'll turn to the world's most influential sermon, Jesus's Sermon on the Mount. Next, we'll consider some of the important parables Jesus told. In chapter 4, we'll turn to John's Gospel, studying the, "I am sayings" of Jesus. In chapter 5, we'll turn to what Jesus said about the meaning of his death. And finally, we'll look to what Jesus said in anticipation of, and then following, his resurrection.

Today 2.4 billion people claim to be followers of Jesus. Another 1.9 billion Muslims hail Jesus as a prophet. Large numbers of people of other faiths, and of no faith, look at Jesus as a "great moral teacher." But beyond a few verses, few seem to know what Jesus actually taught. My aim in this brief volume is to lift up some of the most important things that Jesus said and to invite us to consider what they mean for our lives, in the hope that we might "hear and understand, and bear fruit" (Matthew 13:23).

Chapter 1

The Kingdom of God Has Come Near

Chapter 1
The Kingdom of God Has Come Near

Jesus came to Galilee, proclaiming the good news of God, and saying, "The time is fulfilled, and the kingdom of God has come near; repent, and believe in the good news."

—Mark 1:14-15 (NRSV)

*"You cannot know anything about Jesus, **anything**, if you miss the kingdom of God."*

—Gordon Fee

One Sunday I queried my congregation, "If someone asked you to summarize Jesus's message, what would you say?" They began to shout out answers, most of which were some variation of "Love!"—love God, love your neighbor. Love *is* the central ethic of the Christian faith and the defining mark of the Christian life. But if we want to know the central focus of Jesus's message, of which love is a component, we have to look elsewhere.

For every time in the Gospels that Jesus calls his followers to love, there are four times he mentions the kingdom of God (or as Matthew has it, "the kingdom of heaven," or sometimes just "the kingdom"). In Jesus's first recorded sermon in Mark we read, "The time is fulfilled, and the kingdom of God has come near; repent, and believe in the good news" (Mark 1:15 NRSV).

And even when Jesus does not directly mention the kingdom of God, he is demonstrating some dimension of life in the kingdom, or the ethics of the kingdom, or calling his hearers to be a part of the kingdom. In Luke 4:43 Jesus says, "I must preach the good news of God's kingdom in other cities too, *for this is why I was sent*" (emphasis added).

New Testament scholar Gordon Fee once wrote, "You cannot know anything about Jesus, *anything*, if you miss the kingdom of God. . . . You are zero on Jesus if you don't understand this term. I'm sorry to say it that strongly, but this is the great failure of evangelical Christianity. We have had Jesus without the kingdom of God, and therefore have literally done Jesus in."[1]

If the kingdom of God is the central focus of Jesus's preaching, teaching, and ministry, if it is the reason why he was sent, it seems important for us to understand what he meant by the kingdom of God, and what his teaching about the Kingdom means for us today. To do that, we'll begin by looking at the foundational assertion in Scripture that God is the rightful king or ruler over creation.

God as King

Barukh atah Adonai Eloheinu Melekh ha'olam. These words are used at the beginning of most Jewish prayers and are translated into English as, "Blessed are you, Lord our God, king of the universe." Some Jews prefer to use the word *ruler* or *sovereign* in place of king, but the meaning is the same—God is the rightful ruler over all that exists. I asked a rabbi friend how often he utters the *Barukh Atah* each day. He replied that on a typical day he would say these words one hundred times. *One hundred times* each day he recognizes God as the ruler of the universe, and not only as the ruler of the universe, but as *his* sovereign as well.

The Hebrew words for *king* and *kingdom* both signify reigning, ruling, or having authority or dominion. Many today prefer the phrase *the reign of God* to *the kingdom of God. Kingdom* can imply a particular geographic location, but *God's reign* applies to everything. God reigns over the cosmos, over the laws that govern our universe; God reigns not only over places, but all of creation, not only over nations, but individual human hearts.

The Old Testament repeatedly affirms that God rules as king of the heavens, king of creation, king of the earth, and king of Israel. Look at Psalm 99:1-4.

> *The LORD is king; let the peoples tremble!*
> *He sits enthroned upon the cherubim; let the earth quake!*
> *The LORD is great in Zion;*
> *he is exalted over all the peoples.*

Let them praise your great and awesome name.
Holy is he!
Mighty King, lover of justice,
you have established equity;
you have executed justice
and righteousness in Jacob. (NRSV)

When Jews bless God as king or ruler of the universe, *melek ha'olam*, the Hebrew *ha'olam* can refer to the world or the entire universe, but it can also mean time and eternity. Hence, Psalm 10:16 notes, "The Lord rules forever and always!" The Lord is *melek ha'olam*, the psalmist says.

So, in a sense, everything and everywhere and every time is God's kingdom.

The Great Rebellion

Despite God's rightful place as king of *ha'olam*, Genesis 1:28 tells us God gave humans "dominion" over the earth: "Be fruitful and multiply, and fill the earth and subdue it; and have dominion over the fish of the sea and over the birds of the air and over every living thing that moves upon the earth" (NRSV). Assumed in this dominion-giving was that humans would seek to do God's will; they would recognize they were merely stewards of the earth, ruling on behalf of its Creator.

But that is not what happened. In what is the archetypal story of humanity, the first humans turned away from God's will, and paradise was lost. The story of Adam and Eve's turning from God to eat the forbidden fruit is our story. Our great struggle as humans comes down to the question of whether we will live under God's reign, or whether we'll seek to be our own *melek ha'olam*.

We all find ourselves wrestling, for most of us daily, with the temptation to eat the forbidden fruit in our lives. The classic list of the seven deadly sins captures many of our struggles: lust, gluttony, greed, sloth (or better, indifference), anger or rage, envy, and pride. Each of these might be seen as the temptation to substitute something else in place of God reigning over our hearts and lives. The seven deadly sins are all variations on the theme of idolatry.

We all find ourselves wrestling, for most of us daily, with the temptation to eat the forbidden fruit in our lives.

We see this in societies and nations. Nationalism, including Christian nationalism, substitutes nation and identity, power and politics for living under the reign of God. The various armed conflicts around the world bear the marks of Cain and Abel. We see this in Russia and Ukraine, Israel and Gaza, and in the infighting in the Democratic Republic of Congo, Sudan, and Ethiopia, to name just a few.

These struggles are not new. The Hebrew prophets wrote of the sins of God's people who were perpetually turning away from God. Hosea wrote in the eighth century before Christ,

When Israel was a child, I loved him,
and out of Egypt I called my son.
The more I called them,
the further they went from me.
(Hosea 11:1-2a)

The Book of Isaiah begins with God saying,

Hear you heavens, and listen earth,
for the LORD has spoken:
I reared children; I raised them,
and they turned against me!
(Isaiah 1:2)

The prophetic cries continued against the people, calling them to repent. In Hebrew, repent is *teshuvah,* which also means "to return." This was the cry from the prophets, "Return to your rightful king! Repent!"

The Revolution Jesus Launched

Things were not so different when Jesus began his public ministry. Roman soldiers occupied the Holy Land. Many Jews yearned for God to send a king, a messiah, who would lead a revolution, expelling the Romans and liberating his people from their rule and ultimately ushering in a time of peace. Some, like the Zealots, were ready to take up arms against the occupiers. Others, like John the Baptist and Jesus, believed in a revolution that began in the human heart, as people repented of their sin and turned back to God. Again, we hear this approach in the Gospel of Mark as Jesus began his public ministry with these words, "The time is fulfilled, and the kingdom of God has come near; repent, and believe in the good news" (Mark 1:15 NRSV).

Jesus launched a revolution, to be sure, but it was not one that raised up an army, or somehow ushered in a supernatural imposition of God's will on earth. Instead, Jesus called people to follow him and showed them what it looked like to live as part of God's kingdom. The kingdom of God would come one human heart at a time, as people changed their hearts and minds and submitted to the reign of God in their lives.

The kingdom of God would come one human heart at a time, as people changed their hearts and minds and submitted to the reign of God in their lives.

I once had a terrific Jewish guide as I was leading a group walking in the footsteps of Jesus in the Holy Land. He knew so much about Jesus and, I believe, truly loved him. But he could not believe that Jesus was the Messiah. "Why?" I asked. He said, "Because he did not fulfill the promises of the prophets concerning the Messiah. We still have war and violence and poverty and injustice in our world." His conception of the Messiah, the anointed king the Jewish people hoped for, was that he would come and somehow instantly, supernaturally, transform our world.

I responded, "I can see why you would say that, but that was not Jesus's strategy. Instead he launched a revolution and called his followers to pursue this revolution in each generation. He called them to love their neighbor, and even their enemies; to show mercy, feed the hungry and clothe the naked. He beckoned them to live under the reign of God."

The Already and the Not Yet of the Kingdom

There were several senses in which Jesus spoke of the kingdom of God. He told his disciples that the kingdom of God was near, or at hand. He described it as upon them, or within them. It could be entered into and experienced here and now. Yet it was also something that was emerging, to be prayed and worked for—"Thy kingdom come, Thy will be done in earth, as it is in heaven" (Matthew 6:10 KJV). Finally, the kingdom was a future hope, something that would be fully realized when Christ returned. On that day his people would "Inherit the kingdom that was prepared for you before the world began" (Matthew 25:34).

The reign of God is a current reality throughout the cosmos, as the psalmist says, "The LORD reigns, let the earth… rejoice!" (Psalm 97:1 NIV). But here on earth, where we struggle to do God's will, or to accept the reign of God, it begins within us, as we yield our lives to Christ and join his revolution. The reign of God expands and is experienced on earth, as people do the will of God as Jesus preached it; when we love God and neighbor, live mercifully, act as peacemakers, when we serve others, welcome the strangers, and care for those in need. *And*, Jesus also speaks of a day when he would return, when we will experience the fullness of the kingdom of God, freed from the sorrow and suffering and pain we now experience in this world.

Closing the Gap

In a very real sense, when Jesus speaks of the kingdom of God, he is speaking of the world as God intended it to be, starting with our lives, as they were intended to be.

Many times in my life and work I've drawn upon a simple idea I first heard from Harvard's Ron Heifetz, founding director of the Center for Public Leadership at the Kennedy School, as a way of thinking about the kingdom of God. Heifetz speaks about the importance of seeing the world as it is, and then imagining the world as it was meant to be. He uses a simple diagram to picture it

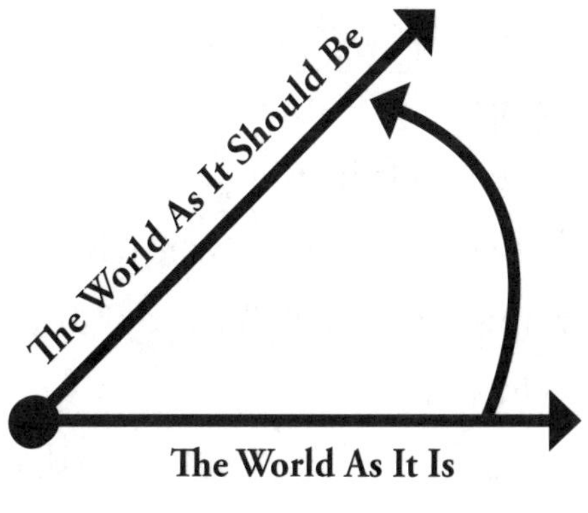

Heifetz notes that our task is to close the gap between the world as it is and the world as it should be. In many ways this is how I see the life of a Christ-follower. In our personal lives, we are, in the words of Alcoholics Anonymous, to take a "fearless moral inventory," seeing our lives, our thought patterns, our habits, our words and actions as they really are. And then, as we consider the words of Jesus, to imagine our lives as they are meant to be if God is reigning in our hearts. And, with the help of the Holy Spirit, to pray and yearn to close the gap.

Likewise, when we consider our family, our community, and the world around us, we're meant to see the reality, the pain, brokenness, injustice, or need, and to imagine, based upon the words of Jesus (and the rest of Scripture) what our families, communities and the world are meant to look like. And our task, as individual Christians and as churches, is to work to close this gap with the power of the Holy Spirit.

A Simple Yet Powerful Example

Anyone can look at the world as it is and imagine the world as it could be if God's will was done. And God has given each of us the ability to close the gap. There's joy found in living this way. At the congregation I serve we ask everyone to be involved in closing the gap. Some do this by visiting the elderly at assisted living and skilled care centers. Others by mentoring children or youth. One dear couple volunteer to help abandoned animals at a local shelter. Some are passionate about helping organize our blood drives or donating blood. We've got teams who visit the prisons as a part of our prison ministry. Others receive training to provide care for people in the hospital.

Ray, Kevin, and Greg are three ordinary guys, Christians at Resurrection who had been involved in our hunger ministry for years (Ray has since moved). They began discussing needs they saw in our city, gaps that needed to be closed. Ray had read Richard Louv's book, *Last Child in the Woods,* about children growing up with a deficit of spending time in nature. Kevin had a brother who worked for the Oregon Sustainable Agriculture Land Trust in Portland, creating urban gardens in open spaces.

Greg is an architect who knew that there were thousands of vacant lots in the urban core of Kansas City.

They began to dream of taking some of those vacant lots to create small orchards. In these orchards children and adults could work together in nature. The orchards would beautify blighted neighborhoods and vacant lots. And they would provide fresh fruit in food deserts. They had a picture of Eden, a bit of paradise they could bring to these neighborhoods.

They pulled together twenty people with different types of expertise to brainstorm and test the idea. They opened their first community orchard in 2012. They called it The Giving Grove. They involved volunteers from various organizations, but ultimately their aim is for neighborhoods to own the orchards and take care of them. Since 2012 they've planted 300 orchards in Kansas City and 250 in other cities across the US. The orchards provide fresh food, opportunities to bring neighbors together, a chance for children to experience nature, and a way for people to beautify their communities. That does sound like a taste of Eden to me.

Three ordinary guys, moved by their faith in Jesus and their desire to not only pray for God's kingdom to come and God's will to be done but also ready to roll up their sleeves and do something about it, launched an organization that has closed the gap for thousands of people. You can find out more at https://www.givinggrove.org.

The work Ray, Kevin, and Greg were doing as volunteers—they each have professional careers—reminded me of a well-known Frederick Buechner quote, "The place God calls you to is the place where your deep gladness and the world's deep hunger meet." This is just one small example of what it looks like when people begin seeing the world through this lens of the kingdom of God and asking how they can close the gap between the world as it is and the world as it is supposed to be.

In Luke 17:20-21, we read, "Once Jesus was asked by the Pharisees when the kingdom of God was coming, and he answered, 'The kingdom of God is not coming with things that can be observed; nor will they say, 'Look, here it is!' or 'There it is!' For, in fact, the kingdom of God is among [or within] you" (NRSV). This idea that the kingdom of God is among us, or within us, points to the reality that the kingdom of God is both about our yielding our lives to God, seeking to do God's will, and a vision for changing the world.

We'll talk about the parables of Jesus in chapter 3, but I want to mention two short parables here. Jesus said to the people,

> *"The kingdom of heaven is like a mustard seed that someone took and planted in his field. It's the smallest of all seeds. But when it's grown, it's the largest of all vegetable plants. It becomes a tree so that the birds in the sky come and nest in its branches.*
>
> *He told them another parable: "The kingdom of heaven is like yeast, which a woman took and hid in a bushel of wheat flour until the yeast had worked its way through all the dough."*
>
> *(Matthew 13:31-33)*

I take Jesus to mean that the kingdom of God is not something that comes by divine fiat, instantaneously, simply by God's command. No, it starts small and comes slowly like a mustard plant growing, or yeast fermenting a batch of dough. And each person who chooses to follow Christ is like the soil in which the mustard seed is planted or the dough that is leavened by yeast. The heart that is yielded and impregnated with a vision of the Kingdom cannot help but produce a life-giving bush, or transform and enliven an entire batch of dough. That's exactly what Ray, Kevin, and Greg experienced with The Giving Grove!

I wonder, in your personal life, are there places you need to close the gap? At sixty, I'm regularly seeing places in my life where I'm not yet the person I believe God longs for me to be. I'm also intentional about looking to see where I can join with others who are seeking to close the gap in my city (Kansas City) or other parts of the world, and occasionally, like Ray, Kevin, and Greg, seeing those gaps myself and asking what role I can play in helping to close them.

In your community or sphere of influence, where do things not yet look like the world as it was meant to be? Where do you see suffering or need or pain or brokenness? What would your community look like if it reflected God's will? And what could you and your friends or family or church do to close the gap between the two?

While he walked on this earth, Jesus healed the sick—and every one of you who are doctors, nurses, medical professionals, you continue that healing work. He cast out demons of mental illness and addiction, and every one of you who work in the mental health professions continue spreading the kingdom of God, liberating the captives. He fed the multitudes, and called us to give food to the hungry, drink for the thirsty, clothing for the naked—and all who provide care and comfort for the immigrant and the sick and give dignity and love to the prisoner expand his Kingdom. Can you see it?

Here's where love comes in. The central ethic of the Christian faith is love. Jesus told his disciples that this was his commandment, that they love one another. He told his disciples the greatest commandments are to love God and love our neighbor. In the Greek language the New Testament was written in, the word most often used for Kingdom love is *agape*. Scholars debate the precise meaning of this word, but it is most often linked to action, doing love, which involves seeking the good of the other. *Life in the kingdom of God is characterized by humans who pursue love: acts of kindness, compassion, mercy, goodness, and more.*

Life in the kingdom of God
is characterized by
humans who pursue love:
acts of kindness, compassion,
mercy, goodness, and more.

Again, Jesus taught his disciples to pray, "Thy kingdom come, Thy will be done in earth, as it is in heaven" (Matthew 6:10 KJV). The Kingdom is not a place, but a way of living in which we seek God's will to be done, and wherever and whenever we do God's will, the Kingdom has come.

We often want God to supernaturally intervene and heal the world of its brokenness, injustice, and pain. To make all things right and to do it right now. But that is not how God generally works. Instead, God calls *us* and empowers *us* with the Spirit, to not only pray for God's kingdom to come and God's will to be done, but to offer ourselves to that end.

REPENT!

I'd end where we began this chapter, with Jesus's first sermon where he announced, "The kingdom of God is at hand." The kingdom of God is still at hand. What should our response be to this message of Christ? He called his hearers to, "Repent!"

Repent is a pretty dramatic word—in Hebrew, as noted above, the word is *teshuva*. It literally means "to return." It implies that someone has taken a wrong turn, gotten lost, strayed from the right path. Can anyone doubt that humanity has, in so many ways, taken a wrong turn? In our own lives, we have done the same.

Jesus spoke Aramaic and Hebrew. He likely used the word *teshuva—return*! But the New Testament was written in Greek, and Mark uses the word, *metanoeite* from *metanoeo,* which means to change your mind, your thoughts and ideas. That change of mind leads to a change of heart, a transformation of one's devotion, commitment, and emotions. And this, in turn, leads to a change of behavior—a changed life. The kingdom of God spreads, one person at a time.

I wonder if you've ever become spiritually or morally lost? Have you strayed from the right path, missed the mark, or turned away from God's will? I have. And on a daily basis, in my morning prayers, I ask for God's forgiveness and yield my life to him once more, pledging to follow God as my king. I pray daily for God's kingdom to come and God's will to be done, in my heart and life, and through me, in whatever small sphere of influence I have, on earth as it is in heaven.

I'm reminded of Luke's account of Jesus's first recorded sermon in his hometown of Nazareth. It appears in Luke 4:18-21, a very short sermon. He was in his home synagogue and was invited to speak. He was handed the scroll from the prophet Isaiah. He opened it to what we know as Isaiah 61, and he began to read,

The Spirit of the Lord is upon me,
because the Lord has anointed me.
He has sent me to preach good news to the poor,
to proclaim release to the prisoners
and recovery of sight to the blind,
to liberate the oppressed,
and to proclaim the year of the Lord's favor.

Luke continues, "He rolled up the scroll, gave it back to the synagogue assistant, and sat down. Every eye in the synagogue was fixed on him. He began to explain to them, 'Today, this scripture has been fulfilled just as you heard it.'"

The Kingdom Jesus was announcing, and embodying as the Messiah, would mean good news to the poor, release for captives, recovery of sight, and liberation.

In the nearly two millennia since Jesus walked this earth, at their best, his followers didn't merely pray, "Thy kingdom come, Thy will be done in earth, as it is in heaven." They sought to live these words. They were and are revolutionaries who loved their neighbors, and even their enemies. They cared for the sick, provided food for the hungry, showed compassion for the hurting, gave hope for the hopeless, and help for the helpless. They fought injustice and championed kindness. And as they did, as individuals and as churches, the kingdom of God was experienced on earth as it is in heaven. Hospitals, schools, colleges, universities, homeless shelters, soup kitchens, prison ministries, food pantries, antislavery and civil rights movements, marches for peace and justice, have all been led by Christians who sought to live as those who longed to see the kingdom of God come on earth as it is in heaven.

And yet, as individual Christians and as a church, we have often failed to live as those who are part of, and ushering in, the kingdom of God. And this is why we regularly must recall the words to Jesus's first sermon, "The kingdom of God has come near; repent, and believe in the good news" (Mark 1:15 NRSV).

These words of Jesus are part of the liturgy in many churches on Ash Wednesday, the beginning of the season of Lent. Lent is the forty-day season of self-examination and penitence leading up to Good Friday and Easter. With ashes we acknowledge our sin and repent, and we remember our mortality as we hear the words "ashes to ashes, dust to dust." Lent reaches its climax on Good Friday when we mark Christ's crucifixion for sin, and Easter when we remember his triumph over sin and death.

Whether you are reading this book as Lent begins, or some other time of year, remember the words of Jesus, and its powerful call to us: The kingdom of God has come near; repent, and believe in the good news.

Chapter 2
The World's Most Important Sermon

Chapter 2
The World's Most Important Sermon

Now when Jesus saw the crowds, he went up a mountain. He sat down and his disciples came to him. He taught them.

—Matthew 5:1-2a

"If I had to face only the Sermon on the Mount and my own interpretation of it, I should not hesitate to say, 'O yes, I am a Christian.' But... in my humble opinion, what passes as Christianity is a negation of the Sermon on the Mount."

—Mahatma Gandhi

If the kingdom of God is Jesus's driving vision, the Sermon on the Mount serves as the road map for how his followers are to live out that vision. In it, Jesus addresses the missional, ethical, and spiritual life of those who seek to live as subjects of God. He speaks as both prophet and shepherd in the three chapters of Matthew that comprise the sermon. Within the Sermon on the Mount, you'll find many of Jesus's best-known and most influential teachings including the Beatitudes, the Lord's Prayer, and the Golden Rule.

The great Methodist missionary to India, E. Stanley Jones, once said, "The Sermon on the Mount seems dangerous. It challenges the whole underlying conception on which modern society is built." World War II General Omar Bradley said of it, we "have grasped the mystery of the atom and rejected the Sermon on the Mount.... Ours is a world of nuclear giants and ethical infants."[1]

English priest and theologian John R.W. Stott wrote, "The Sermon on the Mount is probably the best-known part of the teaching of Jesus, though arguably it is the least understood, and certainly it is the least obeyed. It is the nearest thing to a manifesto that he ever uttered, for *it is his own description of what he wanted his followers to be and to do*"[2] (emphasis added). And Mahatma Gandhi noted, "If I had to face only the Sermon on the Mount and my own interpretation of it, I should not hesitate to say, 'O yes, I am a Christian.' But... in my humble opinion, what passes as Christianity is a negation of the Sermon on the Mount."

Each of these reminds us that while the message of Jesus is clear, it is not easy to live out. And though billions of people have heard of the Sermon on the Mount, many would be hard pressed, without some prompting, to recall most of what Jesus taught there.

While we call it the Sermon on the Mount, it seems likely that this was not a single sermon, but a compilation of Jesus's teachings shared many times in a variety of settings. Luke's version of this message, set not on a mountain, but on the plain, only contains about 30 percent of the material Matthew includes. Even some of the common material found in both Matthew and Luke is recounted somewhat differently (see, for instance, their respective versions of the Beatitudes and the Lord's Prayer).

In this chapter we'll focus on the longer version of the Sermon on the Mount found in Matthew 5, 6, and 7. Like each chapter in this book, we will merely touch on the major themes of the sermon. This material in the Sermon on the Mount easily merits an entire book. And, in fact, this chapter is a bit longer than the others for that reason. When we think of the message of Jesus, the Sermon on the Mount is essential, and I've tried to touch on most of it here. I'd encourage you to have your Bible with you as you read this chapter, reading along as we consider this important compilation of Jesus's teaching.

Before we delve into what Jesus actually said in the Sermon on the Mount, I'd like to say a word about *how Jesus speaks*. In Matthew, Mark, and Luke Jesus speaks prophetically. By this I don't mean that he is telling the future, though occasionally he does foresee the future. Prophetic speech, in the Hebrew Bible or the Old Testament, was less foretelling and more forth-telling—speaking hard truths and challenging the status quo.

These prophetic texts of Scripture were often a bold word, focused on societal and personal sins, and calling people to change—to repent. They speak with a broad brush, offering clear rules for right ethical and spiritual behavior. Prophetic preaching or teaching seldom attempts to address possible exceptions to the rules, though the prophets and Jesus clearly would have known there were exceptions, or nuances, places where more than one ethical or moral rule conflicts with one another.

We also see that while Jesus called people to a holiness of heart and life, a righteousness that exceeded the scribes and the Pharisees, when he ministered with people his actions were characterized by grace and mercy. I think here of his call to avoid adultery and to eschew divorce. Yet he offers living water to a woman married and divorced five times and freely shows mercy to a woman caught in the act of adultery. He was known by his detractors as a friend of sinners. So we read Jesus's high moral and ethical standards in the light of the mercy he showed those who violated these same standards.

A second bit of information that is helpful in understanding *how* Jesus speaks is that he often uses hyperbole; he uses exaggeration to make a point. When someone uses hyperbole, we don't take them literally, we take them seriously. If someone tells you they are so hungry they could eat a horse, they don't literally mean they could or would wish to eat a horse, but they do mean they are very hungry. We'll see, in the Sermon on the Mount and elsewhere in the Gospels, multiple examples of Jesus's prophetic hyperbole. With this in mind, let's consider the world's most important sermon.

The Beatitudes: The Pursuit of Happiness

The Sermon on the Mount begins with the Beatitudes. The word *beatitude* comes from the Latin *beatus* and its family of words, which signify happiness, good fortune, or blessedness. The name *Beatrice* comes from the same word. In Greek the word is *makarios,* which like the Latin signifies a state of happiness.

We spend a great deal of time in our lives chasing happiness. The Declaration of Independence famously notes that humans, "are endowed by their Creator with certain unalienable Rights, that among these are Life, Liberty and the pursuit of Happiness."

When you think of those who are truly blessed, whose lives are happy, and who experience good fortune, what people do you think of? Many picture blessedness as wealth, beauty, popularity, and power.

I was watching the news the morning after the annual Met Gala. Held in New York City each year as a fundraiser for the Metropolitan Museum of Art, this event is the "it" gala that "everyone who is anyone wants to be seen at." The national media cover it. The paparazzi swarm around it. Society's glamorous, including many of Hollywood's A-Listers, arrive in the most dazzling, or sometimes outrageous, attire. I watched as one woman's dress was so form-fitting that she could not walk up the steps and had to be lifted, one step at a time, by her bodyguard! These attendees represent, for many, what it means to be blessed, beautiful, and beatific.

But in the Beatitudes, Jesus offers a very different definition of who the blessed and beautiful are, or will be, in the kingdom of God. He speaks both in the present and future tenses. Those he mentions as blessed or happy now are so because they know and trust what *will be* in the kingdom of God. These blessed and beautiful in the kingdom of God look different from the people likely to be invited to the Met Gala, which is why some refer to Jesus's words as pointing to the "great reversal" in the kingdom of God.

Take a look at who the blessed, happy ones are in the kingdom according to Jesus,

> *Happy [or blessed, or fortunate, depending on the translation] are people who are* ***hopeless****, because the kingdom of heaven is theirs.*
>
> *Happy are people who* ***grieve****, because they will be made glad.*
>
> *Happy are people who are* ***humble****, because they will inherit the earth.*
>
> *Happy are people who are* ***hungry and thirsty for righteousness****, because they will be fed until they are full.*
>
> *Happy are people who* ***show mercy****, because they will receive mercy.*
>
> *Happy are people who have* ***pure hearts****, because they will see God.*
>
> *Happy are people who* ***make peace****, because they will be called God's children.*
>
> *Happy are people whose lives are harassed because they are* ***righteous****, because the kingdom of heaven is theirs.*
>
> *Happy are you when people* ***insult you and harass you and speak all kinds of bad and false things about you, all because of me****. Be full of joy and be glad, because you have a great reward in heaven. In the same way, people harassed the prophets who came before you.*
>
> *(Matthew 5:3-12, emphasis added)*

In the kingdom of God, the invitees to the gala are the poor and the humble, the heartbroken and harassed, the meek and those whose hearts are pure, the peacemakers and the persecuted. In God's eyes, it is these who are the beautiful, who, in the Kingdom, will be comforted, filled; it is they who will inherit the earth and, by faith, already possess the kingdom of heaven.

Jesus's Beatitudes in Luke go a bit further than those recorded in Matthew,

> *Happy are you who are poor,*
> *because God's kingdom is yours.*
> *Happy are you who hunger now,*
> *because you will be satisfied.*
> *Happy are you who weep now,*
> *because you will laugh. . . .*
> *But how terrible for you who are rich,*
> *because you have already received your comfort.*
> *How terrible for you who have plenty now,*
> *because you will be hungry.*
> *How terrible for you who laugh now,*
> *because you will mourn and weep.*
> *How terrible for you when all speak well of you.*
> *Their ancestors did the same things to the false prophets.*
> *(Luke 6:20-21, 24-26)*

This reversal of fortunes in God's kingdom is described throughout Scripture. In Proverbs 3:34 we read, "[God] mocks mockers, / but he shows favor to the humble." This passage is quoted by both James and Peter in the New Testament as, "God stands against the proud, but favors the humble" (James 4:6b and 1 Peter 5:5b).

Mary's Magnificat captures the same idea about God,

He has scattered those with arrogant thoughts and proud inclinations.
He has pulled the powerful down from their thrones
and lifted up the lowly.
He has filled the hungry with good things
and sent the rich away empty-handed.

(Luke 1:51b-53)

What does this mean for those who are blessed with resources, influence, or power *now*? How do the rich avoid being sent away empty? In Matthew 23:11-12, Jesus says, "The one who is greatest among you will be your servant. All who lift themselves up will be brought low. But all who make themselves low will be lifted up." As we'll see in the next chapter, he speaks clearly of giving food, drink, clothing, and care for "the least of these." And in the Beatitudes Jesus says that the peacemakers and the pure in heart; the humble and those who hunger for doing what is right before God; and the merciful—the Greek word signifies compassion—find happiness or blessedness in the kingdom of God.

As an aside, I love Kurt Vonnegut's comment on the fifth beatitude, "blessed are the merciful." While Vonnegut was a humanist, he genuinely loved Jesus and the Sermon on the Mount, from which he often quoted in his books and in his life. In 1999 he gave the commencement address at Agnes Scott College in Decatur, Georgia. In it he said, "If Christ hadn't delivered the Sermon on the Mount, with its message of mercy and pity, I wouldn't want to be a human being. I would rather be a rattlesnake."[3]

The Mission of God's People—Living as Salt and Light

Look next at Matthew 5:13-17 where Jesus begins to map out the mission of those who are part of the kingdom of God. He begins, "You are the salt of the earth." In the days before refrigeration, salt was used to preserve food, to keep it from spoiling. It was also known by many that salt was life-giving, essential for human health. And finally, salt was universally used to enhance the flavor of whatever it touched. It had such value in the ancient world that the Romans sometimes paid their soldiers in salt. Our word *salary* comes from this practice, *sal* being the Latin word for salt.

Imagine asking, before you walk out of the house each day, "How can I enhance the lives of others? How can I bring out the goodness in others and the world around me? How can I be a life-giving, life-preserving force for others?" What a great metaphor for the mission of those living with God as their king!

Jesus goes on to say, "You are the light of the world. A city on top of a hill can't be hidden…let your light shine before people, so they can see the good things you do and praise your Father who is in heaven" (Matthew 5:14 and 16). The *you* is plural—you, *together*, are the light of the world. The word for *good* in the Greek of Matthew's Gospel is *kala*. It means good, but also beautiful. Jesus speaks to his disciples, and to all who call themselves disciples today, calling us to be salt and light as evidenced by good and beautiful works—compassion, kindness, love, mercy, and more.

In 1630, John Winthrop, addressing the Holyrood Church in Southampton, England, shortly before leading his fellow Puritans on the long journey to America, quoted Jesus's words in Matthew 5:14, saying of the new community they hoped to establish in the New World, "We must consider that we shall be as a *city upon a hill.* The eyes of all people are upon us"[4] (emphasis added). The Puritans sought to live as those who accepted God's reign and patterned their lives on the values, ideals, and ethics of the Kingdom.

John F. Kennedy drew from Winthrop's message in a 1961 speech, casting America as a city upon a hill. In the years since, it would be used by many presidents to describe America, but none more than Ronald Reagan who spoke of America as a "shining city on a hill." But when Jesus spoke these words, *he wasn't speaking of a nation*, but of the church, his disciples, who were called to be salt and light, letting their light shine by their good works (Matthew 5:16).

On Martin Luther King Jr. Day weekend in 2010, as I was driving to church for Sunday worship, I was listening to an interview with Rev. Samuel "Billy" Kyles on NPR. Kyles was a friend and associate of Dr. King who was standing with him on the balcony of the Lorraine Motel in Memphis when King was shot and killed by an assassin's bullet.

When host Liane Hansen asked, "How will you mark the King holiday in your homily, your sermon?" Kyles replied,

> I'll be talking about knocking holes in the darkness. It is said that Robert Louis Stevenson was a man who never enjoyed good health. He spent a lot of time in his room even as a child. He was always

> looking out the window. His nurse asked him one day, Robert, what are you doing? He said, I'm watching that old man knock holes in the darkness. She said, what are you talking about?
>
> He would climb up the ladder and light the light, come down, move the ladder to the next pole, climb up, come down, move the ladder. And everywhere he would light a light it appeared to him with his little quick mind that a hole was being knocked in the darkness.
>
> And so I'm suggesting that those of us who have the strength and the ability, we should be knocking holes in the darkness.[5]

I love this metaphor of what Jesus had in mind for his followers, that, individually and as communities, we are to knock holes in the darkness. And this, again, is how the kingdom of God expands on earth as we live the vision, values, and ideals of the Sermon on the Mount.

Actors or Authentic Followers?

Starting in Matthew 5:17, and to the end of the Sermon on the Mount, Jesus calls his disciples to a greater righteousness than was evident among the scribes and Pharisees of his day—religious leaders who were known for their apparent piety. In Matthew 5:20 Jesus notes, "Unless your righteousness is greater than the righteousness of the legal experts and the Pharisees, you will never enter the kingdom of heaven." The rest of the Sermon on the Mount demonstrates what this greater righteousness looks like.

The Pharisees were highly respected for their apparent faithfulness and devotion to God. And many no doubt were devout and pious people. But in the Gospels, Jesus often speaks of Pharisees as hypocrites. The word, *hupokrites* in Greek, means an actor, someone pretending to be something or someone they are not. Hypocritical religion is a religion of façade, a mask one wears rather than a transformed heart. Jesus is calling his followers to a religion that goes deeper than the superficial, that involves the heart, a yielding of one's life to God as king, that results in authentic piety.

Beginning in Matthew 5:21, Jesus will paint for us a picture of this greater righteousness. There he says,

> *You have heard that it was said to those who lived long ago,* Don't commit murder, *and all who commit murder will be in danger of judgment. But I say to you that everyone who is angry with their brother or sister will be in danger of judgment. If they say to their brother or sister, "You idiot," they will be in danger of being condemned by the governing council. And if they say, "You fool," they will be in danger of fiery hell.*

I've officiated at the funeral services for more than a dozen people who took their own lives over the last thirty-five years. Most were young adults. Several of these had been so harassed and bullied on social media they could see no other way to stop the pain. I've known others that did not take their lives, but who were seriously wounded by the cruel words and constant harassment of others. Perhaps not surprisingly, the harassers often went to church and would claim to be followers of Jesus.

Among the passages in Paul that I've committed to memory, and asked the congregation I serve to commit to memory, is

Ephesians 4:29: "Let no evil talk come out of your mouths but only what is useful for building up, as there is need, so that your words may give grace to those who hear" (NRSV). Our words can give grace and build up, or they can tear down and destroy. If we are a part of Christ's kingdom, we refrain from evil talk and name calling. I wonder how our politically polarized world might change if the 65 percent of the population who are Christians might follow Christ's words at election time?

Next, Jesus speaks to how we respond when others have sought to harm us. In Matthew 5:38-48 we read,

> *You have heard that it was said,* An eye for an eye and a tooth for a tooth. *But I say to you that you must not oppose those who want to hurt you. If people slap you on your right cheek, you must turn the left cheek to them as well. When they wish to haul you to court and take your shirt, let them have your coat too. When they force you to go one mile, go with them two. Give to those who ask, and don't refuse those who wish to borrow from you.*
>
> *(Matthew 5:38-42)*

Jesus is quoting an excerpt from Exodus in this passage. It was known as the *lex talionis*, the law of retaliation or revenge. It did not require an eye for an eye and a tooth for a tooth—in other words, it did not require retributive justice. Instead, it insisted that if retribution were to be meted out, it had to be proportional to the harm done, "eye for eye, tooth for tooth, hand for hand, foot for foot, burn for burn, wound for wound, stripe for stripe" (Exodus 21:24-25 NRSV).

Here we see another example of Jesus's prophetic hyperbole. I don't believe he intended that we stand by and let others injure us. His point was that we are to move away from a model of retributive justice where we retaliate against those who harm us. It only leads to continued pain. He calls us to forgiveness rather than retribution.

This section reaches its climax in Matthew 5:43-44, where Jesus says, "You have heard that it was said, *You must love your neighbor* and hate your enemy. But I say to you, *love your enemies* (emphasis added) and pray for those who harass you." Love, here, is not warm affectionate feelings, but practicing loving-kindness and seeking the good of the other. This is among the loftiest of the Kingdom ethics to which Jesus calls us. Do good to, and pray for, those who wrong us.

Paul captures this idea in Romans 12:20-21, which comes from Proverbs 25:21-22: "If your enemies are hungry, feed them; if they are thirsty, give them something to drink." Then he offers this powerful admonition: "Do not be overcome by evil, but overcome evil with good" (NRSV).

Jesus's words in the Sermon on the Mount, echoed in Paul's words in Romans, provide us with the most redemptive and hopeful response to those who frustrate, hurt, or wrong us. This is why Dr. Martin Luther King Jr. found Jesus's message in the sermon to be a compelling road map for the civil rights movement. In his autobiography he noted, "It was the Sermon on the Mount, rather than a doctrine of passive resistance, that initially inspired the Negroes of Montgomery to dignified social action. It was Jesus of Nazareth that stirred the Negroes to protest with the creative weapon of love."[6]

In the remainder of Matthew 5, Jesus applies this same call to a higher righteousness to the question of marriage, adultery, divorce, and to swearing oaths.

In Matthew 5:27-30, Jesus addresses lust and adultery. He says,

> *You have heard that it was said,* Don't commit adultery. *But I say to you that every man who looks at a woman lustfully has already committed adultery in his heart. And if your right eye causes you to fall into sin, tear it out and throw it away. It's better that you lose a part of your body than that your whole body be thrown into hell. And if your right hand causes you to fall into sin, chop it off and throw it away. It's better that you lose a part of your body than that your whole body go into hell.*

Jesus takes the seventh commandment (or sixth, depending on how they are numbered) and makes this commandment infinitely more difficult. Jesus calls us not only to avoid the physical act of adultery, but to avoid desire and lust as well. Infidelity begins in the heart. James 1:14-15 notes, "One is tempted by one's own desire, being lured and enticed by it; then, when that desire has conceived, it gives birth to sin" (NRSV).

Here we have another example of his prophetic hyperbole, both in Jesus's bold statement that lustful thoughts violate the commandment and in his call to chop off our hand, or gouge out our eye if our hands or eyes are causing us to sin. Jesus does not intend us to literally cut off our hands or pluck out our eyes. But we are to hear him as he is saying that the thoughts we entertain can be deadly and lead to pain.

Following his mention of faithfulness in marriage, Jesus addresses divorce. Jesus challenges the prevailing practice among many men in first-century Judaism who interpreted Deuteronomy 24:1 ("Suppose a man enters into marriage with a woman, but she does not please him because he finds something objectionable about her, and so he writes her a certificate of divorce . . . ", NRSV) in such a way that *anything* a husband found displeasing about his wife, such as her cooking, her appearance, or the sound of her voice, was grounds for divorce. Jesus decried this practice and noted the only cause for divorce was a spouse's infidelity.

Again, Jesus speaks prophetically, in a broad statement that does not attempt to address all exceptions to the rule. He does address one exception to his prohibition against divorce, the exception of marital infidelity. But having counseled with many who were in painful marriages, I believe there are other situations that Jesus would recognize as forms of infidelity, a violation of the marriage covenant even if they did not involve adultery.

When a mate is verbally or physically abusive, this is a form of infidelity. When a spouse is continually dishonest, when they bring their mate to financial ruin, or when they ignore the needs of their mate, they have already violated their vows in which they promised, "to have and to hold from this day forward, for better, for worse, for richer, for poorer, in sickness and in health, to love and to cherish, until we are parted by death."[7]

As a pastor I lift up the inviolable nature of the marriage covenant, and the high ideals Jesus articulates for marriage. I call people to pray for and to work at their marriages, to show forgiveness and mercy, and to seek help when they are struggling. At the same time, I recognize that infidelity or unfaithfulness is not only about the marriage bed, but also the marriage vows.

Marriage was intended by God to be a gift, where both people seek to be helpers and companions to one another, not a life sentence of misery and pain.

True Spirituality or Theatrics?

In Matthew 6, Jesus continues the theme of a greater righteousness, but turns his attention to spiritual practices. In verse 1 he notes, "Beware of practicing your piety before others *in order to be seen by them*; for then you have no reward from your Father in heaven" (Matthew 6:1 NRSV, emphasis added). In the verses that follow, he will address acts of generosity to the poor, public prayers, and fasting. He will then address the issue of what we treasure, and finally, the connection between what we treasure and worry.

Jesus calls his disciples to an authentic spirituality.

We've already seen that Jesus addresses the religious leaders, particularly the scribes and Pharisees, as hypocrites—the literal meaning of the word *hupokrites* was acting—pretending to be something they were not. When Jesus challenges his readers not to practice their piety "in order to be seen by others," the Greek word for "to be seen" is *theaomai*. It shares the same Greek root from which we have our word *theatre*. Jesus calls his disciples to an authentic spirituality, not that of an actor on a stage, putting on a performance to gain the accolades of others.

I think about "photo op" piety, when public officials and people running for office do some charitable act just to be filmed or photographed so that others can see them doing this act of piety. Often they are present only long enough to get the photo. But it is not just public officials, or people running for office, for whom this is a problem. Today, Instagram, SnapChat, Facebook, and X all provide opportunities for the rest of us to highlight our acts of piety—a staged piety aimed at gaining the approval or affirmation of others.

There is an interesting tension here, even within the Sermon on the Mount. In Matthew 5:16 Jesus tells us to "Let your light shine before people, *so they can see the good things you do* and praise your Father who is in heaven" (emphasis added). Yet here he tells us to do our acts of piety in private where no one can see you doing it. Which is it? It is both. Jesus is again speaking of motive. Living our faith in such a way that people see an authentic love for God and others is important, it is our witness. But if our aim is affirmation for ourselves, rather than "praise for your Father who is in heaven," we've missed the mark. We have to constantly be watchful of our motives.

There is something in many of us that craves recognition and affirmation, particularly when we are doing something selfless, something overtly for God or others. But when we do this for our own "glory" or to meet our needs for affirmation and praise we fall short. Jesus demands not simply right actions, but right motives. Listen to what Jesus says about acts of generosity toward those in need,

> *Whenever you give to the poor, don't blow your trumpet as the hypocrites do in the synagogues and in the streets so that they may get praise from people. I assure you, that's the only reward they'll get. But when you give to the poor, don't let your left hand know what your right hand is doing so that you may give to the poor in secret. Your Father who sees what you do in secret will reward you.*
>
> (Matthew 6:2-4)

Again, it is literally impossible for our left hand to not know what our right hand is doing, but Jesus is making a powerful point. The highest form of giving seeks no praise or affirmation, but simply seeks to bless the recipient and to honor God.

A woman in my congregation had been very successful in life. During her lifetime she gave away millions of dollars, but she refused to allow her name to be on buildings, or to receive recognition for what she had done. She saw her success as a blessing and her resources as a gift. She eschewed nearly all attempts at recognizing her for her generosity. When she died she left a major gift to our church, with no fanfare or advance notification before she died. The gift was used in catalytic ways to have an impact on the lives of thousands of people. A portion of these funds were used to provide seminary scholarships for young people answering God's call to full-time ministry. I asked her children if we could name the scholarships after their mom, and they said, "Absolutely not. Mom would not approve. She wanted no credit for her generosity, her resources came from God and she was simply seeking to be a faithful steward of the blessings in her life." Even after death, her life reflected the words of Jesus in Matthew 6:2-4.

Jesus calls his followers to do the same when it came to prayer.

> *When you pray, don't be like hypocrites. They love to pray standing in the synagogues and on the street corners so that people will see them. I assure you, that's the only reward they'll get. But when you pray, go to your room, shut the door, and pray to your Father who is present in that secret place. Your Father who sees what you do in secret will reward you.*
>
> *(Matthew 6:5-6)*

I've been to John Wesley's eighteenth-century residence in London, next to the City Road Chapel. In his bedroom there is a kneeler, a personal prayer altar. I've knelt there in prayer thinking, *This is where Wesley knelt in prayer, in his bedroom, not in some very public place to be seen by others, and it was here that the power of the Wesleyan revival was unleashed.*

In this section of the Sermon on the Mount addressing genuine versus false piety, Jesus offers a pattern for prayer that has shaped the lives of billions of people. It is the best known and most often prayed prayer in the world, the Lord's Prayer.

The World's Most Prayed Prayer

Jesus introduces it with these words, "When you pray, don't pour out a flood of empty words, as the Gentiles do. They think that by saying many words they'll be heard. Don't be like them, because your Father knows what you need before you ask" (Matthew 6:7-8). He then lays out the following prayer,

> *Our Father which art in heaven, Hallowed be thy name.*
>
> *Thy kingdom come, Thy will be done in earth, as it is in heaven.*

Give us this day our daily bread.

And forgive us our debts, as we forgive our debtors.

And lead us not into temptation, but deliver us from evil: For thine is the kingdom, and the power, and the glory, for ever. Amen.

(Matthew 6:9-13)

In the late first or early second century editors added the doxology to the prayer: "For thine is the kingdom and the power and the glory for ever, amen." It was likely inspired by 1 Chronicles 29:11, "Yours, O LORD, are the greatness, the power, the glory" (NRSV).

Several years ago I wrote an entire book called *The Lord's Prayer* and here will only mention two ideas. First, this prayer is not about telling God what God does not already know, nor advising God on how to run the universe. Instead, in the Lord's Prayer we are focusing our hearts on the things Jesus asks us to pray for, and inviting God to use us, or work in and through us, that we might become, in some small way, the answer to this prayer. The prayer is intended to *shape our hearts and move us to action.*

Every time we say Thy or Thine, instead of my and mine, we are yielding our lives and our will to God. That is the essence of life in the Kingdom.

Second, this prayer moves us from *my, mine,* and *me* to *us, ours,* and *we*. It moves us from a me-centered faith to a we-centered faith. When we pray the Lord's Prayer, we say "Thy kingdom come, Thy will be done." And every time we say Thy or Thine, instead of my and mine, we are yielding our lives and our will to God. That is the essence of life in the Kingdom.

By the second century, early Christians prayed this prayer three times a day. What if you prayed, and meditated upon these words, even once each day? The beautiful thing about the Lord's Prayer is it captures the spirit of Jesus and has the very words of Jesus. And, most of us already have them memorized.

Money and Worry

Matthew chapter 6 concludes with a focus on the disciple's relationship with money, including idolatry and worry. In Matthew 6:19-24, Jesus tells us not to store up treasure on earth, "Where your treasure is, there your heart will be also" (6:21). He cautions against focusing our eyes, and thus our hearts, on what should not be the focus of our hearts. And then he concludes saying, "You cannot serve God and wealth" (6:24).

It is interesting to me that even in first-century Galilee, where most of Jesus's followers were working-class people, there was a need for Jesus to teach them not to make money their idol. How much more so do we struggle with this in our hyper-materialistic era? The antidote, or perhaps better, vaccine, to the spiritual disease of materialism is generosity. The more freely we give, the less hold money has on our hearts.

This serves as a natural transition to Jesus's words, "Therefore, I say to you, don't worry about your life, what you'll eat or what you'll drink, or about your body, what you'll wear. Isn't life more than food and the body more than clothes?" (Matthew 6:25). He goes on to recognize how much anxiety his hearers carried within them. Many may have lived at a subsistence level, truly wondering where their daily bread would come from, or how they would have enough to provide clothing for their children. But they seem to have carried more fear than they needed to. Jesus was confident they would have enough.

Today, we have more than Jesus's first-century followers could have imagined, yet 63 percent of Americans worry more about running out of money than worry about death.[8] Seventy-two percent of Americans say they stress about money at least once a month.[9] After two thousand years, Jesus's words seem more pertinent today than when he first spoke them. Jesus didn't offer a wealth management course in the Sermon on the Mount. But he did offer two keys to addressing financial worry: the first was to trust that God was able to meet their needs (not necessarily their wants, but their needs). The second, which is one of the most powerful statements in the Sermon on the Mount, is found in Matthew 6:33, "Desire first and foremost God's kingdom and God's righteousness, and all these things [what you will eat, and what you will wear] will be given to you as well."

Logs, Prayer, and the Golden Rule

The Sermon on the Mount concludes in Matthew 7 with some of Jesus's most compelling words. Having described what the greater righteousness of the Kingdom looks like, Jesus speaks to his disciples about a tendency he knew they all were afflicted with, one we struggle with today as well: judging others.

> *Don't judge, so that you won't be judged. You'll receive the same judgment you give. Whatever you deal out will be dealt out to you. Why do you see the splinter that's in your brother's or sister's eye, but don't notice the log in your own eye? How can you say to your brother or sister, "Let me take the splinter out of your eye," when there's a log in your eye? You deceive yourself! First take the log out of your eye, and then you'll see clearly to take the splinter out of your brother's or sister's eye.*
>
> *(Matthew 7:1-5)*

Once more, Jesus goes straight for the heart. The hyperbole is wonderful—a splinter in your neighbor's eye versus the log in your own. We find it so easy to get out the magnifying glass and tweezers when looking at the shortcomings of others. But a clear awareness of our own shortcomings can go a long way in keeping us from giving in to this tendency.

This brief reminder, logs and splinters, helps us show grace toward others. It keeps us from becoming modern-day versions of the judgmental Pharisees with whom Jesus struggled. I'd remind you (and me) that Jesus spoke these words to his own disciples, knowing this would be a problem for *them*, and in the process it would diminish their witness. In Jesus's day, there were many people who were alienated from God and from the synagogue because of the judgmental tendencies of religious people. Jesus, on the other hand, drew these people to himself, scrapping the judgment. What he offered was love and grace. Our job as his followers is not to judge, but to love.

In Matthew 7:7-11, Jesus revisits prayer, reminding his hearers that when we ask, we receive, when we seek, we find, and when we knock, the door is opened. It is an interesting passage. Is Jesus promising here that whatever we ask for, God will miraculously give us? Having spent more than forty years praying daily, I don't believe that is what Jesus is saying. But he is describing God's providence, and how life generally works.

I believe that often our prayers serve as an invitation for God to work in and through us. The Latin phrase *ora et labora*—pray and work—has been helpful to me. We *ask*, and we work, and we often receive. We *seek*, and we work, and we often find. We *knock*, and we work, and the door is often opened to us. I am reminded that we are also God's way of answering the prayers of others. We pray, the Holy Spirit nudges us, and we get to work. I have seen this thousands of times in these years of praying.

And I'm reminded that Jesus said God gives good gifts to those who ask. He doesn't say extravagant gifts. And he doesn't say how God gives us these gifts. Again, it is helpful to remember that we are often God's means for answering other people's prayers.

Jesus concludes this section on prayer in Matthew 7 with the Golden Rule, "Therefore, you should treat people in the same way you want people to treat you; this is the Law and the Prophets" (Matthew 7:12). The Golden Rule is often read to stand alone, apart from what immediately precedes it, and that may be correct. But perhaps it is also the key for understanding how God answers prayer, namely, by God's people doing to others what they would have others do to them. Most often my prayers have been answered through the hand of others who treated me with compassion and care, which I suspect is the same way they would wish to be treated.

Whether that was the reason Jesus's words in the Golden Rule appear here, I cannot be sure, but it should be noted that, in a sense, the "therefore" is in response *to all that Jesus has already said* in the Sermon on the Mount. The Golden Rule is a summary of what Jesus had taught, of the ethics of the Kingdom, and the call to his disciples of greater righteousness. Anger, name calling, adultery, divorce, truth telling, generosity to the poor, and judging others could all be summarized in this one commandment: "Do unto others as you would have them do unto you; this is the Law and the Prophets."

The Golden Rule is a summary of what Jesus had taught, of the ethics of the Kingdom, and the call to his disciples of greater righteousness.

Judgment and the Sermon on the Mount

A pericope is a short section of text, or passage of Scripture, that can stand alone. The Sermon on the Mount is made up of twenty-four or twenty-five pericopes. When we come to the end of the sermon, Matthew has placed together four pericopes, each of which is focused on calling his hearers to choose the better of two paths. Each could have functioned as the end of the message.

In Matthew 7:13-14 Jesus says, "Go in through the narrow gate. The gate that leads to destruction is broad and the road wide, so many people enter through it. But the gate that leads to life is narrow and the road difficult, so few people find it." This is a call to action, a call to choose to pursue the life Jesus has just outlined in the Sermon on the Mount. Jesus notes that this is the harder path; in Robert Frost's famous words, the road is "the one less traveled by" that will make all the difference. Many people choose the path of least resistance, the easy path, the comfortable path. But pursuing the kingdom of God means choosing the narrow path.

In Matthew 7:15-20, Jesus contrasts true prophets with false prophets, good trees and bad trees. He notes that there are some religious people who come in "sheep's clothing" but inwardly are ravenous wolves. Some Christians have a tendency to view other Christians they disagree with through the lens of this passage.

Starting with the Protestant Reformation, there have been Protestants who saw the Pope and other Catholic officials as false prophets. Catholics, in turn, saw Martin Luther and other reformers in the same light. When Billy Graham insisted that his crusades be integrated, he was accused by some of being a false prophet and a wolf in sheep's clothing. Today, those Christians who support the ordination of women or the welcome and inclusion of LGBTQ persons are considered false prophets and wolves in sheep's clothing by those Christians who reject either or both of these ideas.

So, how do we know if someone is a false prophet, a wolf in sheep's clothing, or a faithful follower of Jesus and a true shepherd? Jesus shifts metaphors from prophets and sheep to good and bad fruit trees, saying, "you will know them by their fruit." What does the fruit of a faithful follower of Jesus look like? In the context of the Sermon on the Mount the fruit we will know them by is a life consistent with what Jesus has been teaching.

It is being peacemakers and pure in heart; being humble and hungering to do what is right before God. It is being merciful; showing compassion and demonstrating generosity for the broken, the poor, those in need. The fruit we will know them by is whether they are acting as salt and light and whether they love their enemies and turn the other cheek. The fruit is seen in being faithful to one's spouse. It is practicing piety for the sake of piety, not for show. It is praying *and working* for God's kingdom to come and God's will to be done; it is forgiving sinners and seeking first God's kingdom. It involves taking the log out of one's own eye, and doing unto others as we would have them do unto us. This is the good fruit Jesus expects of the good trees in the Sermon on the Mount.

In Matthew 7:21-23, Jesus notes that there will be some who believed they were his followers to whom he will say on the Judgment Day, "Away from me, I never knew you."

> *Not everybody who says to me, "Lord, Lord," will get into the kingdom of heaven. Only those who do the will of my Father*

who is in heaven will enter. On the Judgment Day, many people will say to me, "Lord, Lord, didn't we prophesy in your name and expel demons in your name and do lots of miracles in your name?" Then I'll tell them, "I've never known you. Get away from me, you people who do wrong."

(Matthew 7:21-23)

It is interesting that the people Jesus turns away on the Judgment Day thought they were his followers. They appear to have been very religious people, they even prophesied in Jesus's name, expelled demons, and did "lots of miracles," again, in his name. But they did not "do the will of" his Father in heaven. When Jesus rejects them, they are quite surprised. They actually thought they were doing God's will. Again, how do we know if we are doing his Father's will? Doing his Father's will means living the Sermon on the Mount. (This passage is similar to another, a parable of judgment we'll explore in the next chapter, the parable of the sheep and the goats in Matthew 25).

Finally, the Sermon on the Mount concludes with words about two different builders, a wise and a foolish one, who built their homes on two very different foundations, bedrock or sand.

Everybody who hears these words of mine and puts them into practice is like a wise builder who built a house on bedrock. The rain fell, the floods came, and the wind blew and beat against that house. It didn't fall because it was firmly set on bedrock. But everybody who hears these words of mine and doesn't put them into practice will be like a fool who built a house on sand. The rain fell, the floods came, and the wind blew and beat against that house. It fell and was completely destroyed.

(Matthew 7:24-27)

The picture is powerful, particularly for anyone who has seen a house destroyed because its foundation failed. Jesus ends this sermon by inviting his hearers to build their home, that is, their life, not on sand, but upon his words as articulated in the Sermon on the Mount.

Entering through the narrow gate, producing good fruit, doing the will of Christ's Father, and building our house on the rock, are all different ways of speaking about living the words of the Sermon on the Mount. And when we live them, the kingdom of God comes, and God's will is done, on earth as it is in heaven.

Chapter 3
Jesus Spoke to Them in Parables

Chapter 3

Jesus Spoke to Them in Parables

He did not say anything to them without using a parable. But when he was alone with his own disciples, he explained everything.

–Mark 4:34 (NIV)

The parables are the characteristic message of Jesus... they are His most rememberable message... they are His most persuasive message; a prosier teaching might not break our stubborn will, but the sight of the father running to welcome his wayward son leaves us "defenseless utterly."[1]

–George Buttrick

I once preached a sermon on manure.

We had two horses at the time, and each evening, before putting the horses away for the night, the stalls would have to be mucked out. With a pitchfork, we'd separate the manure from the clean shavings that lined the stall, toss the manure into a wheelbarrow, and take it outside to the manure pile.

One day I noticed a wildflower growing in the middle of the manure pile. I chuckled and thought, "Now that's a powerful picture of how God works. He takes the 'manure' in our lives—the unpleasant, difficult or crummy things that happen—and, given time, transforms it into fertilizer, bringing good and beautiful things from it." I was reminded of the words of Isaiah 61:3, that God gives us "beauty instead of ashes" (NIV). My entire sermon the next week was built around this analogy. Twenty years later, there are still people who come to talk to me about that sermon, and how it spoke to them.

In essence, the manure and wildflower served as a parable. It was something from everyday life that illustrated a spiritual principle in a way that spoke to people and helped them remember it.

Jesus was a master storyteller who saw spiritual truths illustrated in nature, in human behavior, and in everyday life. The word *parable* is a transliteration of the Greek word *parabole* which means, "to throw alongside." It is a comparison or analogy, aimed at communicating truth, inspiring the heart, or calling people to action. Jesus used parables to explain the heart, character, and will of God and the nature of God's kingdom.

In some ways, Jesus's parables functioned like riddles, requiring hearers to ponder the parable with open hearts and minds before the meaning was clear. At times even his disciples required him to explain their meaning.

Depending on what you count as a parable, there are somewhere between thirty and fifty parables found in the Gospels.

Some are very short comparisons. Some are much more detailed short stories. New Testament scholar C. H. Dodd noted, "At its simplest, the parable is a metaphor or simile drawn from nature or common life, arresting the hearer by its vividness or strangeness, and leaving the mind in sufficient doubt about its precise application to tease it into active thought."[2]

In Matthew 13:33 we find an example of a short parable, an analogy, that prompted hearers to ponder what Jesus meant: "The kingdom of heaven is like yeast, which a woman took and hid in a bushel of wheat flour until the yeast had worked its way through all the dough." What do you think he meant by this? It is a bit of a riddle, and, like poetry, might lead to differing interpretations but largely in the same vein. Look up different commentators and you might find somewhat different interpretations.

In the parable above we're meant to notice that the woman *hid* the yeast in a *bushel* of flour. *Hid* likely points to the fact that though the yeast is nearly invisible, it is an active agent transforming the dough. The mention of a bushel of dough is surprising, this is enough to make sixty one-pound loaves of bread! That's a lot of bread, providing sustenance for many. Notice the woman too. Is she God, or does she represent us, as we seek to mix the yeast of the Kingdom into our everyday lives?

In a sense, the parable may be making a similar point to two of the metaphors Jesus used in the Sermon on the Mount. There he called his followers to be salt, positively transforming all that we touch, and light, giving light to all around us.

The genius of Jesus's use of these kinds of parables is that they force hearers to engage with the parable, to think about and ponder their meaning.

While many of Jesus's parables were relatively brief and slightly enigmatic, some of his most beloved parables were stories whose meaning seemed more immediately evident to his hearers. In the remainder of this chapter, we'll consider three of the best-known parables of Jesus.

The Parable of the Sheep and the Goats

Matthew 25 contains three parables of judgment that climaxes in the parable of the sheep and the goats. Jesus begins painting a picture of the final judgment:

> *Now when the Human One [Son of Man] comes in his majesty and all his angels are with him, he will sit on his majestic throne. All the nations will be gathered in front of him. He will separate them from each other, just as a shepherd separates the sheep from the goats. He will put the sheep on his right side. But the goats he will put on his left.*
>
> *(Matthew 25:31-33)*

The rest of the parable will paint a picture of the criteria Christ will use at the Last Judgment when he judges "the nations." Some Christians are very uncomfortable with this parable. There is no mention of Christ's atoning death for our sins or justification by faith. The parable, taken at face value, teaches that the sole criteria for salvation is our works, specifically how we cared for the hungry, the thirsty, the stranger, the naked, sick, and the imprisoned:

> *Then the king will say to those on his right, "Come, you who will receive good things from my Father. Inherit the kingdom that was prepared for you before the world began. I was hungry and you gave me food to eat. I was thirsty and you gave me a drink. I was a stranger and you welcomed me. I was naked and you gave me clothes to wear. I was sick and you took care of me. I was in prison and you visited me."*
>
> *(Matthew 25:34-36)*

Likewise, those who are condemned are condemned precisely because they failed to care for the hungry, the thirsty, the stranger, the naked, the sick, and the imprisoned.

Some have sought to resolve the theological dilemma by suggesting that the parable concerns those who have not heard the gospel, and they will be judged by these criteria. Some suggest "the least of these" (vv. 40, 45) is Christian missionaries, and that the pagans who welcomed these missionaries welcomed Jesus in whose name they came. Perhaps.

I wonder if a better explanation is to note that parables are not meant to carry the entire gospel. Analogies and parables break down in points, and Jesus speaks in prophetic hyperbole, even in his parables. This parable points to something very important, but it does not contain everything Jesus wants us to know about God's kingdom.

Which of us could ever be certain we had done enough to care for the poor or to welcome the strangers or visit the sick and imprisoned? How many times will we have failed at that in our lifetimes? We still need grace and atonement. But Jesus is teaching, as he did in the Sermon on the Mount, the importance of being merciful. He is demonstrating, as he did in the Beatitudes, his concern for the hopeless, the meek, and the lowly. He is pointing, once more, to the "great reversal" in the Kingdom, to what it looks like to humble oneself, to not only pray for God's kingdom to come and for everyone to have daily bread, but to actually work to see this happen. He is showing how we become the answer to other people's prayers. And, in this parable, he is demonstrating that our mercy and compassion for those who struggle *matters a great deal to God.*

Our mercy and compassion
for those who struggle
matters a great deal to God.

This parable points to what life in the kingdom of God is meant to look like. It looks like humans caring for one another—acting as one another's "keepers," to quote the story of Cain and Abel (Genesis 4:9 NRSV). And the parable is meant to shake us out of resignation and indifference to the suffering of others, calling us to action.

The Parable of the Good Samaritan

Let's shift to Luke's Gospel. Luke records more parables, and more unique parables, than the other Gospels. I've noted elsewhere that among Luke's major emphases is Jesus's concern for the outsiders, outcasts, and outlaws.[3] We see this emphasis in so many of the parables Luke records, including the two we'll consider in the remainder of this chapter, the parable of the good Samaritan and the parable of the prodigal son.

In both of these parables we'll see that Luke helps us understand the meaning of the parable by telling us the context in which Jesus tells it. Further, and this is true of many of the parables of Jesus, these parables will contrast two or more characters and invite us to ask, *which character in the parable am I?*

The parable of the good Samaritan is recorded in Luke 10:25-37. Luke sets up the parable by noting, "A legal expert stood up to test Jesus. 'Teacher,' he said, 'what must I do to gain eternal life?'" Jesus fields a lot of questions in the Gospels, and he asks quite a few as well (Jesus asks 305 questions in the Gospels to be exact!). He often responds to questions with other questions, which is what happens when Jesus replies to the man's question with two questions: "What is written in the Law? How do *you* interpret it?" (v. 26, emphasis added).

The religious legal expert (scribe) responded, "*You must love the Lord your God with all your heart, with all your being, with all your strength, and with all your mind, and love your neighbor as yourself.*" Elsewhere Jesus calls these the two great commandments on which the law and the prophets hang. Jesus affirms the scribe's response saying, "You have answered correctly. Do this and you will live."

Then Luke tells us, "But the legal expert wanted to prove that he was right, so he said to Jesus, 'Who is my neighbor?'" It is in response to this question, to the legal expert's desire to know who is and who is not his neighbor, who he does and does not have to love, that Jesus tells the story of the good Samaritan.

Leviticus 19:18 is the source of the command to love one's neighbor. The verses around it make clear that Israelites were called to love their fellow Israelites. Perhaps the man wanted to see if Jesus agreed, or if he might narrow the circle, requiring love only for one's immediate family and friends, or one's literal neighbors. Perhaps he wondered if Jesus would widen the circle to include non-Israelites.

There's something in most of us that wants to know who we don't have to love. I once attended a church that was excellent at caring for their fellow church members. They did a magnificent job of providing food for single moms who struggled in their congregation or visiting those in the hospital or ensuring that everyone in the church felt loved. But their care stopped at the church doors. They never engaged in serving the poor or helping those in need outside their church; they never felt compelled to address the economic disparities in their city.

Another church I knew, back in the sixties in Kansas City, was quite willing to serve others in the community, regardless of the color of their skin. They saw this as their "Christian duty." But when the pastor announced one Sunday to this all-white congregation that they would henceforth welcome "Negroes" into the church, one of the largest adult Sunday school classes left, en masse, to join another church that would ensure the "separation of the races." The first church failed to understand how all encompassing "neighbor" was. The Sunday school class at the second church failed to fully understand what it meant to love.

In response to the religious expert's question, Jesus began his parable, "A man went down from Jerusalem to Jericho. He encountered thieves, who stripped him naked, beat him up, and left him near death" (v. 30).

You can still see portions of the ancient Roman road that ran from Jerusalem to Jericho. It is a seventeen-mile journey that descends 3,300 feet from Jerusalem that sits at 2,500 feet *above* sea level, to Jericho, which sits at 800 feet below sea level. It ran along Wadi Quelt, a beautiful, rugged, and treacherous canyon where there were plenty of places for bandits to hide and accost those making the journey.

Jesus had the attention of everyone in the crowd as he was telling this story. Those who had traveled that road knew of its dangers. The traveler, presumably a Jew, was near death. Surely someone would come to help him. You likely remember what happened next in Jesus's story,

> *Now it just so happened that a priest was also going down the same road. When he saw the injured man, he crossed over to the other side of the road and went on his way. Likewise, a Levite came by that spot, saw the injured man, and crossed over to the other side of the road and went on his way.*
>
> *(Luke 10:31-32)*

We might think of Levites as worship leaders, though they served many other functions in the religious life of the Jewish people. Both the priest and the Levite were religious leaders not unlike the legal expert who had asked Jesus the question. Both of them saw the naked and nearly dead stranger and sought to avoid him, walking to the other side of the road.

Two thousand years later, we can easily imagine this story unfolding in our time. We can imagine religious leaders and ordinary Christians who look the other way, rather than stopping to help someone in need. Perhaps we ourselves have "crossed over to the other side of the road."

In his last sermon, the night before he was murdered, Dr. Martin Luther King Jr., was preaching on this parable. It was April 3, 1968, and Dr. King was in Memphis, Tennessee, to support the city's striking sanitation workers. In February of that year, two sanitation workers, Echol Cole and Robert Walker, were crushed to death by the malfunctioning of the garbage compactor in the back of their trash truck. The sanitation workers were striking for safer working conditions and a living wage. King had already been in Memphis twice in March and was now back once again to stand with the city's 1,300 sanitation workers.

That night, before a packed house at Mason Temple, King gave what has become known as his "Mountaintop" speech. At one point he recognized the many clergy who had shown up to march with the strikers, including Billy Kyles, mentioned in chapter 2. Then he began to talk about the parable of the good Samaritan. I believe he spoke about this parable because it was the lens through which he saw the strike, his role, and the role of all who came alongside the strikers, advocating on their behalf. Echol Cole, Robert Walker, and all the city's sanitation workers were the "certain man" who had been beaten and robbed and left for dead, in this case by an unjust system.

Unlike the priest and the Levite, King and his fellow clergy and the thousands of others who had stood with the sanitation workers in their strike were seeking to be like that Samaritan whom Jesus made the unlikely hero of his story. They were like the good Samaritan, who "came to where the man was. But when he saw him, he was *moved with compassion*" (emphasis added).

Jesus's parable continued, showing what real mercy and compassion look like—not merely a feeling, but a course of action,

> *The Samaritan went to him and bandaged his wounds, tending them with oil and wine. Then he placed the wounded man on his own donkey, took him to an inn, and took care of him. The next day, he took two full days' worth of wages and gave them to the innkeeper. He said, "Take care of him, and when I return, I will pay you back for any additional costs."*
>
> *(Luke 10:34-35)*

Dr. King spent a few moments pondering why the priest and Levite didn't stop to help. He gave the standard answers: perhaps they were in a hurry to get to a meeting, or they knew that touching a dead body would make them ritually unclean. And then he notes that perhaps, on this treacherous road from Jerusalem to Jericho, they were aware that there was some inherent danger in stopping to help the man. Maybe it was a trap. Or maybe those who accosted this man might be nearby and accost them as well.

Then King offered such a marvelous line that I have repeated many times when preaching this parable. It seems, King speculated, that the religious leaders each asked the question,

"What will happen to me if I stop to help this man?" "But then the good Samaritan came by. And he reversed the question: '*If I do not stop to help this man, what will happen to him?*'"

King had had death threats regarding his coming to Memphis to march with the strikers. Upon boarding the plane for Memphis there was a bomb threat called in for the plane which required deplaning and searching for a bomb. These were no doubt on his mind that night when he devoted several minutes to talk about his own death, what was prescient in the light of his assassination the next day. He chose to take the risk the Good Samaritan did to help the Jew who had been beaten and left for dead as he walked the road to Jericho.

Jesus concluded his parable by turning to the religious scribe and asked, "What do you think? Which one of these three was a neighbor to the man who encountered thieves?" Only the Samaritan, of the three who encountered the man left for dead that day, rightly understood who his neighbor was, and what it means love your neighbor as yourself. The scribe rightly noted that it was the Samaritan who acted as neighbor. Which led Jesus to say to him, "Go and do likewise."

As you may know, the relationship of Jews to Samaritans in Jesus's day was not so different from that of Jews and Palestinians today. Jesus made the "other," the disdained Samaritan who had compassion for the Jew, the hero of this story. The Samaritan lived the great command to love your neighbor.

Luke wants to make sure we ask, Who am I in this parable? I know at times, moved by fear, not so much the fear of possible danger, but simply fear of the opinions of others, I've been the priest or the Levite. Jesus's words in this parable compel me to want to be the good Samaritan. That is the power of a parable.

Luke wants to make sure we ask, Who am I in this parable?

The Parable of the Prodigal Son

That leads to a one final parable to consider in this chapter, the parable of the prodigal son. Like the good Samaritan, this parable only appears in Luke's Gospel.

We find the context for Jesus's telling of this parable in Luke 15:1-2, "All the tax collectors and sinners were gathering around Jesus to listen to him. The Pharisees and legal experts were grumbling, saying, 'This man welcomes sinners and eats with them.'" Before the parable even begins, we see a contrast between two sets of characters: the "tax collectors and sinners" gathered around Jesus, and the Pharisees and scribes, watching and grumbling about the company Jesus kept.

What ensues are three parables Jesus tells, in each of which he is trying to speak to both the "sinners" and the "saints." They capture Jesus's own mission, "to seek out and to save the lost" (Luke 19:10 NRSV), and the heart, character, and will of God. He hopes to remind the "sinners" that they are loved and wanted by God. He hopes to remind the "saints" of what it means to be good shepherds of God's flock. (See Ezekiel 34 where God expresses his disappointment in Israel's shepherds who forgot to care for God's sheep.)

In the first of these three parables, Jesus describes a shepherd who had one hundred sheep. One of them wandered away. Jesus asks, "Wouldn't he leave the other ninety-nine in the pasture and search for the lost one until he finds it? And when he finds it, he is thrilled and places it on his shoulders" (Luke 15:4-5). He notes the shepherd's joy at the one lost sheep that was found. The implication: God is like that shepherd, and the tax collectors and sinners are like that lost sheep.

Then Jesus tells of a woman who lost a valuable coin, likely worth a day's wages. She searches high and low to find that coin and rejoices when she does. The implication: God is like that woman, and sinners are like that lost coin (Luke 15:8-10).

As the climax of these parables, Jesus begins,

> *A certain man had two sons. The younger son said to his father, "Father, give me my share of the inheritance." Then the father divided his estate between them. Soon afterward, the younger son gathered everything together and took a trip to a land far away. There, he wasted his wealth through extravagant living.*
> *(Luke 15:11-13)*

LaVon and I have been saving for retirement since we were in our early twenties, sacrificing so that we might be prepared for our "golden years." We anticipate that at the end of our lives we'll give a portion of our estate to the church and other causes, but we'll also give some to our children and any grandchildren we have. But at this point, we don't know for certain that we'll have enough to cover all of our medical costs in retirement. If one of our girls came to us today, and wanted her portion of the inheritance, it would be bad form. I hope we have something to give them someday, but we may need it between now and then. That's what this younger son was asking of his father.

What is worse, he went to a land far away and squandered it all on extravagant living (*prodigal* means extravagant, wasteful, or reckless). I wonder how many in that crowd of tax collectors and sinners listening to Jesus could see themselves in the younger son? Maybe they'd struggled with selfishness, made poor decisions, taken advantage of a parent, or lived recklessly? And surely many of the Pharisees and scribes also saw these sinners as the prodigal son.

Jesus heightens the tension in the story when he said,

> *When he had used up his resources, a severe food shortage arose in that country and he began to be in need. He hired himself out to one of the citizens of that country, who sent him into his fields to feed pigs. He longed to eat his fill from what the pigs ate, but no one gave him anything.*
>
> *(Luke 15:14-16)*

What do you think the crowd was saying now? Surely they could identify, even if they had not personally made such a mess of their lives, they knew some who had. And the religious leaders, can you hear their thoughts? "Serves him right! What a terrible son. He's getting what he deserves."

Then Jesus captures a moment we often call, "hitting bottom."

> *When he came to his senses, he said, "How many of my father's hired hands have more than enough food, but I'm starving to death! I will get up and go to my father, and say to him, 'Father, I have sinned against heaven and against you. I no longer deserve*

to be called your son. Take me on as one of your hired hands.'"
So he got up and went to his father.

(Luke 15:17-20a)

Perhaps you'll remember from chapter 1, that the Hebrew word for repentance, *teshuva*, means "to return." That is precisely what this boy is doing. He has sinned—gone astray. But now he seeks to return home.

At this point, everyone is wondering how Jesus will conclude this story. The son had acted disrespectfully toward his father and then wasted his father's hard-earned retirement funds. Even the prodigal son only expected to be received as a hired hand or a slave, surely not as a son.

But listen to how Jesus describes the father's response to seeing his son walking home, downcast, in the distance: "While he was still a long way off, his father saw him and was *moved with compassion*. His father *ran to him*, *hugged him*, and *kissed him*" (emphasis added). This is unthinkable to the religious leaders. This father was being reckless, prodigal, with his grace. How will the boy learn anything if he is not appropriately disciplined? And where is the justice in this father's response to his son?

But if you looked at the crowd of sinners and tax collectors, I suspect you would have seen tears streaming down their faces. This is what they wished their earthly fathers had been like. But many are also beginning to see precisely what Jesus is really talking about. He is describing their heavenly Father.

Jesus continues, "Then his son said, 'Father, I have sinned against heaven and against you. I no longer deserve to be called your son.'" Here the act of "returning" is coupled with regret, confession, and a clear awareness of the consequences of his sins. Once more, Jesus offers a stunning response from the boy's father,

> *But the father said to his servants, "Quickly, bring out the best robe and put it on him! Put a ring on his finger and sandals on his feet! Fetch the fattened calf and slaughter it. We must celebrate with feasting because this son of mine was dead and has come back to life! He was lost and is found!" And they began to celebrate.*
>
> *(Luke 15:22-24)*

In essence, Jesus is saying to the crowd of both sinners and saints, "This is what your Father in heaven is like!" Can you imagine just how powerful and compelling this was to the sinners and tax collectors? They could never unhear Jesus's words in this parable. They are words for you too. No matter how far you've gone, no matter how awful your life, you can always come home. And your Father loves you. He wants you. He's been waiting for you to come home! He will celebrate your return home.

No matter how far you've gone,
no matter how awful your life,
you can always come home.

The only people who were not celebrating were the religious leaders. It was this picture of God that Jesus painted with his stories that seemed so inconsistent with the God they preached, who required the blood of animals to atone for sin, whose righteous wrath was deserved by all, but particularly the sinners that surrounded Jesus.

I am reminded of Jonathan Edwards (1703–1758) and the picture of God he painted in his famous sermon, "Sinners in the Hands of An Angry God:"

> *The God that holds you over the Pit of Hell, much as one holds a Spider, or some loathsome Insect, over the Fire, abhors you, and is dreadfully provoked; his Wrath towards you burns like Fire; he looks upon you as worthy of nothing else, but to be cast into the Fire.*

But this is not the picture of God that Jesus conveys in this parable! Jesus called people to repent—to return to the God who loved them.

At this point the Pharisees may well have been shaking their head in disbelief, accusing Jesus of being "soft on sin" and preaching "cheap grace." But Jesus's parable is not over. Now it's time to address the concerns of these religious leaders, who are represented by the older brother in the parable,

> *Now [the father's] older son was in the field. Coming in from the field, he approached the house and heard music and dancing. He called one of the servants and asked what was going on. The servant replied, "Your brother has arrived, and your father has slaughtered the fattened calf because he received his son back safe and sound."* ***Then the older son was furious****.*
>
> *(Luke 15:25-28a, emphasis added)*

I love this part of the parable, which is often ignored by preachers. Here, Jesus speaks directly to the Pharisees and religious leaders. Unlike other places where Jesus calls out their hypocrisy, here Jesus speaks with understanding and compassion for the older brother.

It was not hard to understand why the older brother was angry, just as it was not hard to understand the religious leaders' frustration at Christ's demonstration of extravagant mercy to sinners. It did seem unjust and unfair. This portion of the parable reminds us of another parable Jesus told, in Matthew 20:1-16, the parable of the workers in the vineyard. There the owner of a vineyard hires workers throughout the day. At the end of the day he decides to give each worker the same wages, even though some worked only an hour and some worked all day. There, too, God's grace seemed unfair. Listen to how Jesus articulates the older son's grievance against his father,

> *Look, I've served you all these years, and I never disobeyed your instruction. Yet you've never given me as much as a young goat so I could celebrate with my friends. But when this son of yours returned, after gobbling up your estate on prostitutes, you slaughtered the fattened calf for him.*
>
> *(Luke 15:29-30)*

Everyone standing near Jesus, both the "sinners" and the "saints," must have been nodding their head. The extravagant, wasteful, prodigal grace of the father seemed unfair to all of them, though quite welcome to the sinners. You could imagine the older son, and the religious leaders too, saying, "Punish the little brother. Let him come back as a servant, but not as a son. Welcome him back if you must, but don't slaughter the fattened calf for him!"

In Jesus's parable, the father responds to his elder son's anger with understanding and compassion. He first begs the boy to come into the house to join the party, and then he says, "Son, you are always with me, and everything I have is yours. But we had to celebrate and be glad because this brother of yours was dead and is alive. He was lost and is found" (Luke 15:31-32).

Of course, God's mercy seems unfair. But just as the father in the parable has not forgotten the faithfulness of the oldest son; so, too, God has not forgotten the faithfulness of those earnest religious leaders, nor of all who faithfully serve God their entire lives. But if they understand the depth of God's love for his children, they, too, will eventually come to celebrate when the brother or sister who was lost has been found again. In so many ways the religious leaders got it right, but in one important area they had become blind, failing to understand the love and mercy of God for his lost children.

In Jesus's life and ministry, he continually painted this picture of the extravagant love and mercy of God. In Luke 7, it is "a woman from the city, a sinner" (v. 37) (most have imagined her the town prostitute) who weeps at Jesus's feet, to whom he freely offers love and grace. In Luke 19 it is Zacchaeus, a chief tax collector. Jesus showed mercy and befriended a man who was known by all to have been of bad character. And, at the very end of his life, Jesus tells a criminal dying on the cross next to him (in Luke 23, the Greek word *kakourgous* describes him—he was an "evil doer"), "today you will be with me in paradise" (v. 43).

Of all the things I love about Jesus, it is this I love the most. It is the reason I am a follower of Christ. It is what I hope to demonstrate in my life and ministry. It is why, in 1990, my wife and I and our two children started a church whose passion is to reach *nonreligious and nominally religious* people.

Today, Christianity is often more associated with the spirit of the Pharisees and the older brother of Jesus's parable. That spirit pushes away the very people Jesus came to search for and save (Luke 19:10). How grateful I am that Jesus showed us a very different picture of God: One who holds the high expectations of the Sermon on the Mount and the extravagant grace of the prodigal's father.

In the parable of the prodigal son, where do you see yourself?

Jesus was a master storyteller. His stories moved people. They challenged norms, shed light on the nature and character of God, and made plain God's will for the lives of his hearers. Two millennia later, the parables continue to speak with power to us today.

Chapter 4
Who Do YOU Say that I Am?

Chapter 4

Who Do YOU Say that I Am?

Jesus said . . .
I am the bread of life.
I am the light of the world.
I am the gate of the sheep.
I am the good shepherd.
I am the resurrection and the life.
I am the way and the truth and the life.
I am the true vine.

–John 6:35; 8:12; 10:7-11; 11:25; 14:6; 15:1

The Fourth Evangelist held his faith deeply, and he clearly wanted his readers to share his passion for life shaped by the incarnation. He weaves together narrative and theology in an attempt to open up the wonder and mystery of the incarnation . . . [He] loved God and Jesus deeply, and he invites his readers to share that love.

–Gail R. O'Day[1]

At one point in his ministry, Jesus asked his disciples this question: Who do people say that I am? They replied, "Some say John the Baptist, others Elijah, and still others one of the prophets." Then he asked another question, "Who do *you* say that I am?" There was silence this time, like when a teacher asks a question you think you know the answer to, but you're too afraid to say it, in case you are wrong. Only Peter had the courage to speak up this time: "You are the Christ" (Mark 8:27-29, emphasis added).

John does not record this episode in his Gospel, but it feels like he spent the next fifty years thinking about the question and perhaps remembering his silence when Jesus asked it. And his Gospel is one long reply.

Up to this point we've focused on Matthew, Mark, and Luke in our quest to hear the message of Jesus. We've learned about the kingdom of God, we've studied the Sermon on the Mount, and we've considered several of Jesus's parables. But in John's Gospel, Jesus barely mentions the kingdom of God (just four times, compared to the one hundred plus times in Matthew, Mark, and Luke). He gives no equivalent of the Sermon on the Mount. And though Jesus deploys lots of metaphors in John, the Gospel doesn't record a single parable of Jesus.[2]

What John does do, again and again and again, is to record things Jesus said that would point to the answer to two questions: Who is Jesus? and What difference does he make in the lives and communities of those who believe in him?

John was likely the last Gospel written. The early church fathers say it was written by John, the "beloved disciple" of Jesus, in his latter years. He seems less concerned with writing a biography of Jesus than ensuring that his readers could answer the questions above. And, in some ways, it feels like John is finally blurting out the answer he wished he'd given on that day near Caesarea Philippi when Jesus asked his disciples who they thought he really was. Only now, he's had a lifetime to reflect upon it.

John opens his Gospel with a dramatic prologue. Listen to just the first few verses,

In the beginning was the Word
and the Word was with God
and the Word was God.
The Word was with God in the beginning.
Everything came into being through the Word,
and without the Word
nothing came into being.
What came into being
through the Word was life,
and the life was the light for all people.
The light shines in the darkness,
and the darkness doesn't extinguish the light.
(John 1:1-6)

Who do you say that I am? You are the Word of God, God's will and desire to be revealed to humanity, wrapped in human flesh. Who do you say that I am? You are the one through whom all things came into being. Who do you say that I am? You are life! You are light, a light that shines in the darkness that the darkness can't snuff out!

That's just the beginning of the Gospel of John, but it points to what scholars describe as John's "high Christology." Christology is the study of the identity of Jesus. A low

Christology emphasizes Jesus's humanity, his role as a teacher. A high Christology emphasizes the idea that Jesus was not merely a man, but that he was also divine. Matthew, Mark, and Luke allude to Jesus's divinity. But in John, nearly every page associates Jesus with God and points to God's work in and through him to rescue humanity.

Often John records Jesus describing who he is and his association with God. For example, in John 10:30, Jesus declares, "I and the Father are one." In John 14:9-10, when Philip asks Jesus, "Show us the Father," Jesus replies, "Don't you know me, Philip, even after I have been with you all this time? Whoever has seen me has seen the Father. . . . I am in the Father and the Father is in me" (John 14:9-10).

John includes lengthy dialogues Jesus has with others, dialogues not typical of the other Gospels. And in these dialogues, Jesus often reveals who he is. The vocabulary, grammar, and syntax of Jesus in John is markedly different from his way of speaking in Matthew, Mark, and Luke, which has led many scholars to see John as paraphrasing Jesus, or placing words on his lips that reflect the truth about Jesus as John came to see him over the decades. Whether they were in every case the literal words, or paraphrases, or capture the theological reflections of John, they point to John's answer to the questions, Who is Jesus? and What difference does he make in the lives and communities of those who believe in him?

The I Am Sayings in John

Among the most interesting, cryptic, yet compelling ways in which Jesus answers the question of his identity and significance in John's Gospel is with two small words, "I Am." In order to make sense of how these words reveal the identity of Jesus in John, we've got to first turn to the story of Moses and the burning bush, one of the most important stories in the Bible.

In Exodus chapter 3 we find Moses tending sheep in the Sinai. One day he stumbles upon a bush that is burning but not consumed by the fire. Stopping to examine this curious sight, God speaks to him from the bush, saying, "I've clearly seen my people oppressed in Egypt. I've heard their cry of injustice because of their slave masters. I know about their pain.... So get going. I'm sending you to Pharaoh to bring my people, the Israelites, out of Egypt" (Exodus 3:7, 10).

Shocked and afraid, among other things, Moses says to the Voice calling him, "If I now come to the Israelites and say to them, 'The God of your ancestors has sent me to you,' they are going to ask me, 'What's this God's name?' What am I supposed to say to them?" (Exodus 3:13).

The question was understandable; there were hundreds of deities in the Egyptian pantheon.[3] In essence, Moses was asking, "Which of these deities are you? Are you Osiris or Horus or Amon or Re or one of the other deities?"

God responds to Moses in this cryptic way, "I Am Who I Am. So say to the Israelites, 'I Am has sent me to you'"[4] (Exodus 3:14). There are two Hebrew words used in Exodus 3 to signify God's name, both variations of the verb "to be." The one that will, henceforth, be used as God's name is four letters in Hebrew, *YHWH*, and usually pronounced in English "Yah-way." This name for God appears over six thousand times in the Old Testament, but you would never know it in reading most English translations of the Bible. Jews, concerned with dishonoring God's name, stopped saying it eons ago. When they come across God's name in Scripture, rather than risking besmirching God's name, they will simply say, in Hebrew, *ha Shem* which means, "the Name." Or they will substitute the Hebrew word for Lord—*Adonai*. English translators tend to follow this convention and so, when the Hebrew name for God, *YHWH*, appears in the Old Testament, most English translations substitute, in small caps, "the Lord."

As an example, take a look at Psalm 23. Notice the word Lord appears in both the first and last sentence of the Psalm: "The Lord is my shepherd . . . I will live in the Lord's house as long as I live" (vv. 1, 6). In Hebrew it says, "YHWH is my shepherd. . . . I will dwell in the house of YHWH forever." Again, over six thousand times this name for God appears in the Old Testament.

But what does this cryptic name even mean? Why would God reveal his name as, "I Am"? Jews and Christians have debated the significance of this name for generations, likely since God first uttered it to Moses. I believe that by revealing his name as YHWH God was saying, "I Am Being Itself," or "All-That-Exists-Exists-Because-of-Me." *YHWH* is the Source and Sustainer of everything. Everything is contingent upon God.

This sounds very much like John 1:3, "Everything came into being through the Word, and without the Word nothing came into being." It reminds me of Acts 17:28 where Paul quotes the ancient Cretan Epimenides, saying of God, "In God we live, move, and exist."

When the Hebrew Bible was translated into Greek in the ancient world, Exodus 3:14, "I Am Who I Am" was translated into Greek as *ego eimi ho on*—I Am the One Who Is. *Ego eimi* literally means, "I am." It can simply mean I am and nothing more, as when Jesus says, "I am sending you out..." or "I am gentle and humble in heart..." he likely means nothing more than I am. Even when *ego eimi* stands alone it can be translated as "it is I," or "I am he." But at times, particularly in John's Gospel, when Jesus says *ego eimi* he seems to mean more than that—he seems to be identifying himself with YHWH. But even then, it is not always completely clear and you'll find differences in various translations. Let's take a look at two different groups of I Am sayings in John.

When I Am Stands Alone

In John 4, Jesus meets a Samaritan woman at a place called Jacob's Well. Jesus offers her "living water." The woman then says to Jesus, "I know that Messiah is coming..." and then, according to the Common English Bible translation, "Jesus said to her, "I Am—the one who speaks with you'" (John 4:26). Other translations, like the New International Version (NIV), and New Revised Standard Version (NRSV) translate *ego eimi* here as "I am he." The NRSV typically includes a footnote saying, "*I Am.*"

In John 6, the disciples were in a boat at night in the midst of a storm. Jesus had remained on land. Seeing their distress, Jesus came walking to them on the water. When they saw him they were terrified. It was then that Jesus said, "I Am. Don't be afraid." (John 6:20 CEB). But the NIV and NRSV translate this phrase as "It is I. Don't be afraid." Both the CEB's "I Am" and the NRSV and NIV's "It is I" are possible translations, but for reasons I'll share below, I think the CEB is the better translation here.

In John 8, Jesus is having a conversation with a group of Pharisees. In verse 24 he says to them, "If you don't believe that I Am, you will die in your sins." They respond by asking, "Who are you?"—a loaded question in John whose entire Gospel is focused on answering this question. In verse 28, the CEB has Jesus say to them, "When the Human One is lifted up, then you will know that I Am." Once more the NIV and NRSV have "I am he." But later in the same chapter, when some of his opponents invoke Abraham as their father, Jesus says, "Before Abraham was, I Am" (v. 58). Here the NIV and NRSV join the CEB in translating this, "I Am."

At the last supper in John, Jesus foretells his betrayal by Judas and then he says, "I'm telling you this now, before it happens, so that when it does happen you will believe that I Am" (John 13:19). The CEB and NIV have "I Am," while the NRSV has "I am he."

Finally, in John 18:4-5, when the guards have come to arrest Jesus he asks them, "Who are you looking for?" They replied, "Jesus the Nazarene." To which Jesus replies, "I Am." John notes, "When he said, 'I Am,' they shrank back and fell to the ground" (18:6). Jesus struck terror in the hearts of this "company of soldiers," armed and mighty, when he spoke these two words. He identifies himself again as I Am in verse 8. Once more, the CEB has "I Am" while the NRSV and NIV have, "I am he."

In each of these cases, the translators for the Common English Bible have seen all of the above uses of *ego eimi* by Jesus as a nod to his identification with YHWH. This is in keeping with John's prologue where Jesus is identified as the divine Word, as well as John 10:30, "I and the Father are one," and John 14:9-10, "Whoever has seen me has seen the Father. . . . I am in the Father and the Father is in me." Jesus is the embodiment, the Incarnation, of the One who is the Source-and-Sustainer-of-All-Things.

Before leaving these examples I want to mention a further reflection on John 6:20, when Jesus comes walking on the water to rescue his disciples while they are in a boat in the middle of the Sea of Galilee in the midst of a storm. I love this story, in part because it is a picture of what Jesus still does in our lives as we trust in him.

Job 9:8 says that God alone, "trod the waves of the Sea." In Psalm 77:19 the psalmist speaks to God saying, "Your way went straight through the sea; / your pathways went right through the mighty waters. / But your footprints left no trace!" In walking on water, Jesus has done what Scripture says God alone can do. Jesus goes on to quiet the storm. This power to calm storms, too, is attributed to God in Scripture: Psalm 107:29 says, "God quieted the storm to a whisper; / the sea's waves were hushed," and Psalm 93:4 notes "Mightier than the sea's waves, / mighty on high is the LORD [YHWH]!"

Shortly before her death, I visited my mother-in-law, Bernice, in her care center. She was a part of my life since I was 14, and I loved her dearly. She was struggling with dementia. Her fears became more pronounced as she approached bedtime. Among the scriptures that comforted her was the story of Jesus walking on the water. She pictured Jesus saying to her, as he did to the disciples in the boat that night, "I Am. Don't be afraid." She imagined Jesus stepping into the boat that was her room at the assisted living center. She focused on this story, believing that Jesus was God's very presence coming to her in the darkness, the storm that raged in her mind began to dissipate, and the waves of anxiety began to calm. This story, and repeating the words, "Jesus is in the boat with me," helped her find peace. As I left her that day, she said to me, "I just want to keep remembering that Jesus is in the boat with me. He's in the boat with me right here."

I have heard similar stories from so many other people who picture Christ walking on the water, coming to them in the storm, and calming the wind and the waves.

The Classic Seven I Am Statements

That leads to the seven "I am sayings" of Jesus where Jesus completes the sentence with a predicate noun. Each answers the questions, Who is Jesus? and What is his significance for the lives of those who believe? Here, whether *ego eimi* is simply I am, or I Am, each statement points to divine attributes that he embodies and divine action that he incarnates. All are rooted in the identity and action of God in the Hebrew Bible/Old Testament. These seven are:

- I am the bread of life. (John 6:35, 41, 48)
- I am the light of the world. (John 8:12, 9:5)
- I am the gate of the sheep. (John 10:7, 9)
- I am the good shepherd. (John 10:11)
- I am the resurrection and the life. (John 11:25)
- I am the way, the truth, and the life. (John 14:6)
- I am the true vine. (John 15:1, 5)

Let's briefly consider each.

I Am the Bread of Life (John 6:26-70)

There is no more basic need in life than food and drink. Stop eating and your body begins consuming stored fats. Continue to not eat and your body starts consuming your own muscles. Without food you become fatigued, nauseated, even confused. Your body lacks the nutrients it needs to survive. Within forty-five to seventy days of not eating, you'll die.

Bread is among the most basic of foods—just flour, salt, water and yeast. Even the mention of bread in Scripture is a metaphor for food, for the nourishment we need to survive. It came to represent essential nourishment or sustenance. When the Israelites had been liberated from slavery in Egypt, and lived in the Sinai for forty years, God provided bread for them in the form of manna. God provided just enough each day, a practice intended to remind the Israelites that God was the source of their lives. Manna came to symbolize God's provision for God's people and their dependence upon God for life.

Having just fed five thousand hungry people with five barley loaves and two fish, Jesus makes the first of the seven I Am... statements: **I am the bread of life.** John refers to Jesus's miracles as "signs" because they always point to something deeper. In this case, Jesus provided food for the multitudes, just as God, through Moses, provided manna to the Israelites. But it is more than that.

In Deuteronomy 8:3, Moses said to the Israelites, "One does not live by bread alone, but by every word that comes from the mouth of the Lord [YHWH]" (NRSV). Moses was pointing to the existential, spiritual needs of human beings. We need to know we are loved, we are not alone, that there is meaning to our lives, a purpose for us to fulfill, and so much more. These deeper needs we have are met by "every word that comes from the mouth of the Lord." Once more I'm reminded of John's prologue, "In the beginning was the Word." and "The Word became flesh and made his home among us" (vv. 1, 14).

Jesus fed the multitudes with a miraculous multiplication of bread and fish; but for John, this was a sign of something deeper. Jesus himself, and our belief in and ongoing relationship with him, is the bread that nourishes our soul. Without him, we become spiritually fatigued, confused, weak—spiritually malnourished.

One additional thing to note. John doesn't record Jesus's words about the Eucharist spoken at the Last Supper, despite devoting five chapters to the events of that evening. No, John introduced the Eucharist here, in the dialogue that follows the feeding of the five thousand. After saying, I am the bread of life, he continues,

> *I assure you, unless you eat the flesh of the Human One and drink his blood, you have no life in you. Whoever eats my flesh and drinks my blood has eternal life, and I will raise them up at the last day. My flesh is true food and my blood is true drink. Whoever eats my flesh and drinks my blood remains in me and I in them.*
>
> *(John 6:53-56)*

This was a perplexing statement to the crowds and led many to stop following Jesus (John 6:66). But those Christians reading the Gospel knew precisely what Jesus was talking about. When they gathered together, they shared a meal of bread and wine. The bread and wine of the Eucharist represented Jesus's body and blood. In eating it they were inviting him to dwell in them. They were seeking to be nourished by him who is the bread of life.

Christ is to our soul what physical bread or food is to our body.

Christ is to our soul what physical bread or food is to our body.

Years ago, I lived next door to an older couple who were faithful Catholics. Every morning, they drove to their Catholic church to receive the Eucharist. By this act they were expressing their love for Christ and their yearning to remain in him and he in them. It was beautiful and holy. I don't receive the Eucharist each morning, but when I awaken, I slip to my knees and invite

Christ to be my daily bread, to fill me and nourish me. Likewise at each meal, as I say my mealtime grace, I stop to recognize Jesus as the living bread that gives me life.

Who is Jesus and how does faith in him transform us? He is the bread of life, and our faith in him and our participation in the Eucharist nourish our souls. And, as his followers, we're meant to offer bread to others, literal food as he did to the five thousand who were hungry, but also offering the bread we find in Jesus to a world that is spiritually malnourished.

I Am the Light of the World (John 8:12-59)

Our next I Am saying is found in John 8:12 and 9:5 where Jesus says, **I am the light of the world.** In John 7:2 we read that the setting for this statement is the Festival of Booths (Sukkoth). Jesus makes his way to Jerusalem for the festival that commemorates the Israelites' sojourn in the Sinai for forty years. Exodus 13:21 tells us that during the Israelite's time in the wilderness "The LORD [YHWH] went in front of them in a pillar of cloud by day, to lead them along the way, and in a pillar of fire by night, to give them light, so that they might travel by day and by night" (NRSV). God was literally a light for them during their sojourn in the wilderness.

In Jesus's day, during this festival, there were four seventy-five-foot-tall pillars or lampstands erected in the Temple courts. Atop each were four lamps, sixteen lamps in total, that were lit during a ceremony called, "The Illumination of the Temple." These were a reminder of how God was present with the Israelites in the wilderness as a column of light or fire. He dispelled the darkness and illuminated the way for them. Psalm 119:105 draws upon this same idea when it says, "Your word is a lamp before my feet / and a light for my journey." Again, John has said that in Jesus, "the Word became flesh."

Jesus stood in the Temple during Sukkoth, surrounded by these giant columns with their oil lamps, and said, "I am the light of the world. Whoever follows me will never walk in darkness but will have the light of life" (John 8:12). Darkness is mentioned 173 times in the Hebrew Bible, often representing frightening or hopeless times, times of grief and loss, or moments when people have turned away from God, or when they are utterly lost.

In his prologue, John wrote, "In him was life, and the life was the light of all people. The light shines in the darkness, and the darkness did not overcome it" (John 1:4-5 NRSV). Every year at Christmas Eve candlelight services, the lights of the sanctuary are turned off, and one small candle is lit and brought to the front of the room. We remember that God came to us, born of the Virgin Mary, to bring light to our lives and to our world. We pass the candlelight from person to person until the room is filled with light. The act of receiving that light is an invitation for Christ to illuminate our darkness, and to use us to, in the words from Billy Kyles's sermon in chapter 2, "knock holes in the darkness."

Who is Jesus? He is the light of the world, a light that cannot be extinguished, who illuminates our darkness and calls us to be light for others.

I Am the Gate of the Sheep (John 10:1-9)

Some years ago I was exploring the Judean wilderness with my friend, Palestinian Christian Wissam Saalsa. We came across a series of caves with rocks piled up like a stone wall around the entrance. There was an opening several feet across. It was clear that sheep had recently inhabited the cave.

He said that the Bedouin grazed their sheep in this area, but to protect them from wild animals at night, they brought them into these caves. They built the stone wall to keep the sheep in. Then Wissam sat in the opening that formed the entrance in the stone wall. He noted that the shepherd, with his body, acts as the gate through which the sheep entered this place of safety. And, by his presence, the shepherd keeps wolves and jackals from entering the makeshift sheep pen and harming the sheep. In the morning, the shepherd leads his sheep out of the cave to graze for the day.

It was a graphic portrayal of what Jesus meant when he said, **I am the gate of the sheep.**

Jesus went on to say, "Whoever enters by me will be saved, and will come in and go out and find pasture. The thief comes only to steal and kill and destroy. I came that they may have life, and have it abundantly" (John 10:9-10 NRSV).

Who is Jesus? He is the gate by which we enter God's pasture and protection. He protects us from the "thief"—the evil one who would harm us—and seeks to give us abundant life.

I Am the Good Shepherd (John 10:11, 14)

Just after saying, "I am the gate," Jesus continues, "**I am the good shepherd.** The good shepherd lays down his life for the sheep" (John 10:11 NRSV, emphasis added).

Throughout the Hebrew Bible God describes himself as Israel's shepherd. And the people understood they were his sheep. Psalm 100:3 (NRSV) notes, "Know that the Lord [YHWH] is God. / It is he that made us, and we are his; / we are his people, and the sheep of his pasture."

As a backdrop to Jesus's claim that he is the "good shepherd," there stands a history of Israel's shepherds failing to care for the sheep.

In 586 BC the Babylonians destroyed Jerusalem and took many of the Jewish people captive into exile. Shortly after this God spoke to the religious and political leaders of the Jewish people, now living in exile, chastising them saying,

> *To Israel's shepherds who tended themselves! Shouldn't shepherds tend the flock? You drink the milk, you wear the wool, and you slaughter the fat animals, but you don't tend the flock. You don't strengthen the weak, heal the sick, bind up the injured, bring back the strays, or seek out the lost; but instead you use force to rule them with injustice. Without a shepherd, my flock was scattered; and when it was scattered, it became food for all the wild animals.*
>
> *(Ezekiel 34:2b-5)*

Then YHWH proclaims, "I will seek out the lost, bring back the strays, bind up the wounded, and strengthen the weak" (Ezekiel 34:16). Finally, God promises, "I will appoint for them a single shepherd, and he will feed them" (Ezekiel 34:23). In saying, "I am the good shepherd" Jesus was both identifying with God, who is the Shepherd of us all, but he was also identifying himself as the single shepherd that God promised to send, the Messiah.

I sat with a man in hospice recently. His life had been marked by his struggle with alcoholism. He was divorced and had alienated his son. He had lost most of the friends he had. And because he had not taken care of his health was dying far before his time. He felt alone, misunderstood, and he said he'd never felt loved in all his life. He certainly could not fathom that anyone, at this point, could love him.

When I went to visit him, my prayer was that I might incarnate Christ's love for him. Because he'd been alienated from God, I wanted to gently share with him the story of Jesus, the Good Shepherd whose love and passion was for the lost, the broken, the weak and wounded. I reminded him that he really was loved, and that the Good Shepherd was ready to welcome him back home.

But I was not the only one to do this. I watched his son, whom he had alienated, showing tender care for him. And his ex-wife showed such kindness to him, helping in any way she could and reminding him that he was loved. It was remarkable to watch this unfold. Each were the hands and feet and heart and voice of Christ, the Good Shepherd, walking with him "through the valley of the shadow of death" so that he would "fear no evil."

Jesus is the Good Shepherd who strengthens the weak, heals the sick, binds up the injured, brings back the strays, and searches for the lost.

Jesus is the Good Shepherd who strengthens the weak, heals the sick, binds up the injured, brings back the strays, and searches for the lost.

I Am the Resurrection and the Life (John 11:25)

In John 11, Jesus's dear friend, Lazarus, dies. Jesus arrives several days after his death. Upon his arrival, Lazarus's sister, Martha, blurts out her disappointment with Jesus. And it is in that context that Jesus offers our next I am statement.

> *Martha said to Jesus, "Lord, if you had been here, my brother wouldn't have died. Even now I know that whatever you ask God, God will give you."*
>
> *Jesus told her, "Your brother will rise again."*
>
> *Martha replied, "I know that he will rise in the resurrection on the last day."*

> *Jesus said to her, "**I am the resurrection and the life.** Whoever believes in me will live, even though they die. Everyone who lives and believes in me will never die."*
>
> *(John 11:21-26, emphasis added)*

And then, to make this point clear, Jesus asks to be taken to Lazarus's tomb. He asks that the stone at the mouth of the tomb be rolled away, and he shouts, "Lazarus, come out!" And to the shock of all present, Lazarus came stumbling out of the tomb.

In the week I wrote this, I officiated at the funerals of two parishioners I dearly loved. They were friends who died a week apart. Their families and friends grieved their loss. But both women had such deep faith and had spent their lives following Jesus. We shared these words of Jesus from John 11, as we do at every funeral service—they are a part of our funeral liturgy. And these words temper our grief. They allow us to grieve as people who have hope.

Who is Jesus? He is one who promises to raise us up at our deaths and to give us life.

I Am the Way, the Truth, and the Life (John 14:6)

In John 14, Jesus is with his disciples at the Last Supper, and he seeks to prepare them for his imminent arrest and crucifixion. Jesus tells them, "Don't be troubled. Trust in God. Trust also in meme" (v. 1). And then he speaks of his "Father's house" that has "room enough to spare" and how he is going there to prepare a place for them. We'll come back to these words in chapter 6. For now I want to focus on what he says next.

In John 14:4 he says to his disciples, "You know the way to the place I'm going." Perplexed, Thomas said to him, "Lord, we don't know where you are going. How can we know the way?" (John 14:5). To which Jesus replies, "**I am the way, the truth, and the life.** No one comes to the Father except through me" (John 14:6, emphasis added).

The Book of Acts records that Christians were called followers of "the Way" (Acts 9:2; 19:9, 23; 24:14, 22). The word *way* in Greek, *hodos*, literally means a road or a path. You'll recall that in the Sermon on the Mount Jesus spoke of a wide road that leads to destruction and a narrow gate and difficult road that leads to life (Matthew 7:13-14). Jesus's life, his teachings, his death and resurrection are the way to the Father. Likewise, he himself, as the Word that became flesh, is the truest of truths about God, about life, about being human. And not simply in the sense of eternal life, but in being fully alive here and now, Jesus is life.

The second part of John 14:6, "No one comes to the Father except through me," is interesting and requires a brief comment. Some take this to mean that all non-Christians will go to hell. That is one possible interpretation but seems inconsistent with much of Scripture.[5] Another possible understanding of these words is that anyone who receives salvation, grace, mercy, and life from God will have done so through Jesus whether they are conscious of this or not. If Jesus is God's Word enfleshed, as John asserted, and if Jesus and the Father are one, as he asserted, then any who experience God's providence, any who know God's love, any who find God's peace, any who are granted eternal life, will have received these through Christ, again, regardless of whether they are conscious of it or not.

Jesus is not *a* way, or *a* truth, or one possible path to life. He is *the* way, *the* truth, and *the* life. He is the Incarnation of the I AM, "The Source and Sustainer of Life."

Who is Jesus? He is the way, the truth, and the life, through whom we know God.

I Am the Vine (John 15:1, 5)

Last among the seven classic I am statements are Jesus's words in John 15:1, "**I am the true vine**, and my Father is the vineyard keeper" (emphasis added). He repeats this in 15:5, "**I am the vine**; you are the branches. If you remain in me and I in you, then you will produce much fruit. Without me, you can't do anything" (emphasis added).

If you are a follower of Jesus, you are one of these branches, and the branches on a vine are meant to bear fruit. But that is only possible if the branches remain connected to the trunk.

In the Hebrew Bible, Israel is at times portrayed as a vine (see Isaiah 5:7, 27:2), and God as the vineyard owner or vineyard keeper (see Jeremiah 2:21). Jesus shifts the metaphor here a bit. God is still the vine grower—the vigneron—but in John 15, Jesus is the vine—the roots and trunk—and those who believe and remain in him are the branches. If you are a follower of Jesus, you are one of these branches, and the branches on a vine are meant to bear fruit. But that is only possible if the branches remain connected to the trunk.

Last spring I had an apple tree that had just begun to bloom when the wind from a strong storm snapped off one of its large branches. Surprisingly, the tree's buds continued to open as the branch lay on the ground, and it looked very much alive, but only for a few days. Soon, the fact that it was severed from the tree and disconnected from its source of nutrients saw the buds and leaves begin to wither and quickly die. What a powerful metaphor for what happens to our spirit, and our spiritual lives, when we are disconnected from Christ.

As the time for his crucifixion drew near, Jesus felt an urgency to teach his disciples that as branches they are intended to bear fruit; but to bear fruit, they must remain in him, his life, his teachings, his Spirit. This abiding in Jesus is what is meant when Christians talk about having a relationship with Christ. We talk to him, we offer our lives to him, we listen to and meditate upon his words, we seek to do his will. And we invite his Spirit, the Holy Spirit, to work in us.

What of the fruit they are to produce? Starting in John 15:9, Jesus gives them the command to love one another. And in verse 16 he says, "I chose you and appointed you so that you could go and produce fruit and so that your fruit could last. As a result, whatever you ask the Father in my name, he will give you. I give you these commandments *so that you can love each other*" (John 15:16-17, emphasis added).

Who is Jesus? He is the source of our spiritual life, giving us what we need to bear fruit.

More than fifty years before the Gospel of John was written, Jesus had asked his disciples, "Who do you say that I am?" The entirety of John's Gospel, and particularly Jesus's words recorded in it, seek to answer that question. John wants his readers to see that Jesus is the bread of life. He is the light of the world. He is the gate by which we find protection and the good shepherd who cares for us. In the face of death, he is the resurrection and the life. In a confused world, he is the way, the truth, and the life. He is the vine, and we are his branches, and only if we remain in him we will bear much fruit.

Chapter 5
Final Words

Chapter 5
Final Words

[Jesus said to his disciples,] "I give you a new commandment: Love each other. Just as I have loved you, so you also must love each other. This is how everyone will know that you are my disciples, when you love each other."

—John 13:34-35

Within minutes [the disciples] were bickering over who of them would end up the greatest. But Jesus intervened: "Kings like to throw their weight around and people in authority like to give themselves fancy titles. It's not going to be that way with you. Let the senior among you become like the junior; let the leader act the part of the servant."

–Luke 22:24-26 (MSG)

There is something poignant about a person's last words—the phrases uttered with one's last breaths create meaning that outlives the person who speaks them.[1]

–Strive Newsletter

If you knew you only had days or perhaps hours to live, what would you want to say to your closest friends and family?

I have visited with many people who were approaching death, hundreds I think, over the last thirty-six years as a pastor. One man was dying because of ALS, which had afflicted him earlier than most. He had a wife and two young boys. The two of us sat on his back porch on a warm summer day, and he told me, very carefully articulating his words as the disease had made it difficult for him to talk, the things he wanted me to share with his wife and his sons at his funeral. He was sharing with me what would be his final words to them.

The Gospels record the final words and messages of Jesus. He knew he was going to Jerusalem to die. We might anticipate, as was the case with that young father dying, that Jesus had things he wanted to make sure to say before he died, words that would continue to speak after he was gone. In this chapter we'll explore Jesus's message during the last week of his life, during the last day, and during the final hours.[2]

The Last Week

Jesus entered Jerusalem on the day Christians call Palm Sunday. It was five days before the Passover festival was set to begin. He entered riding a donkey down the Mount of Olives. This was the only time the Gospels record him riding a donkey. He was giving his disciples, and the crowds, a sign. The prophet Zechariah, hundreds of years before Jesus, wrote,

Rejoice greatly, Daughter Zion.
Sing aloud, Daughter Jerusalem.
Look, your king will come to you.
He is righteous and victorious.

He is humble and riding on an ass,
on a colt, the offspring of a donkey.
(Zechariah 9:9)

Some understood instantly what Jesus was doing. They ran to tell their friends, "Jesus of Nazareth is riding a donkey! This is it! The revolution is starting!" Crowds began to gather along the road down the Mount of Olives. They cut down branches, a sign of victory in battle. And they began to shout, "Blessings on the king who comes in the name of the Lord. Peace in heaven and glory in the highest heavens" (Luke 19:38, echoing Psalm 118:26a)

These were dangerous, rebellious words. They implied a new king was coming into town, that the insurrection was underway, just as Passover was set to begin. Luke records, "Some of the Pharisees from the crowd said to Jesus, 'Teacher, scold your disciples! Tell them to stop!' He answered, 'I tell you, if they were silent, the stones would shout'" (Luke 19:39-40).

Yet he was not coming to liberate the Jewish people from Roman occupation. He called on his followers to defeat their enemies with love, not with armed rebellions. No, he came to call all people to change their hearts and lives, to live according to God's will, with God as their king, the very things he'd been teaching and preaching since he began his ministry.

If you'd looked into his eyes that day, you would have seen not joy but sadness as the people shouted their hosannas. He knew what lay ahead for him, but his greater sadness was what lay ahead for Jerusalem and the Jewish people as they pursued armed revolt against the Romans in the decades that would follow his death.

Luke writes,

> *As he came near and saw the city, he wept over it, saying, "If you, even you, had only recognized on this day the things that make for peace! But now they are hidden from your eyes. Indeed, the days will come upon you, when your enemies will set up ramparts around you and surround you, and hem you in on every side. They will crush you to the ground, you and your children within you, and they will not leave within you one stone upon another; because you did not recognize the time of your visitation from God."*
>
> *(Luke 19:41-44 NRSV)*

He was speaking of the destruction of Jerusalem that would occur during the Great Jewish Revolt of AD 66–73, as insurrectionists sought to overthrow Roman rule.

Upon entering the city, he immediately went to the Temple, the place he had called "my Father's house." Listen to how Mark describes what happened next,

> *After entering the temple, he threw out those who were selling and buying there. He pushed over the tables used for currency exchange and the chairs of those who sold doves. He didn't allow anyone to carry anything through the temple. He taught them, "Hasn't it been written,* My house will be called a house of prayer for all nations? *But you've turned it into* a hideout for crooks."
>
> *(Mark 11:15-17)*

This one act would have shocked everyone, enraged the merchants and religious leaders, and ensured that, before the week was out, Jesus would be put to death.

But this act also captured the revolt Jesus was leading, a revolt against a superficial piety that failed to yield one's heart. It was a rebellion against religion that took advantage of people for personal gain. It was a rejection of hypocritical religion that had driven so many away from God.

Each day that week, Jesus returned to the Temple teaching. Throngs came to hear him, while the religious authorities came to question him, test him, and hopefully trap him in his own words. Jesus told parables that were thinly veiled attempts to make clear the sins of the religious leaders. He fielded their questions and masterfully avoided their traps. He became increasingly frustrated with the religious authorities and they with him. In Matthew 23, we read Jesus openly challenging and condemning the "legal experts and Pharisees," unveiling their spiritual pride and hypocrisy. Here he utters the "seven woes" against them, "Woe to you, scribes and Pharisees, hypocrites!" (NRSV).

In Matthew 24, as Jesus and the disciples left the Temple, he took up the theme, once again, of what he foresaw would be the fate of Jerusalem in the years ahead. He said to his disciples regarding the Temple, "Do you see all these things? I assure you that no stone will be left on another. Everything will be demolished" (Matthew 24:2). This was a shocking statement and one that would be used against him at his trial.

Then Jesus spoke of these terrible events in more detail, describing the events that would unfold with the Great Jewish Revolt against the Romans that began in AD 66. In response to the revolt, the Romans sent their legions and crushed the rebellion, sacking Jerusalem, destroying the Temple, killing as many as a million Jews and taking seventy thousand away as slaves to Rome. No wonder Jesus wept as he contemplated these events as he entered Jerusalem on Palm Sunday. Jesus's words in Matthew 24, Mark 13, and Luke 21, what are sometimes referred to as the "Little Apocalypses," describe not only the destruction of Jerusalem in AD 70, but also conflate this with a future "second coming" and the day of the Final Judgment.

In Matthew 25, Jesus tells three parables of judgment to describe what it means to "be ready" for his return and the final judgment. We've already touched on one of these, the parable of the sheep and the goats.

I want to be ready each day, to face suffering if need be, for my faith. I want to be ready always to meet Christ at my death. And should he return and gather the nations before him to separate the sheep from the goats, I want to be ready for that too.

There are some Christians who believe we are living in the "last days." They read passages in the Old Testament, and these apocalyptic passages in the Gospels, along with a smattering of Paul and the Apocalypse of John (Revelation), and they see the signs. While I disagree with their interpretation of these scriptures, I believe their point, and clearly Jesus's point, is to be ready. None of us know how long we will live, when we will die, or when Christ will return and God will put an end to the world as we know it. I want to be ready each day, to face suffering if need be, for my faith. I want to be ready always to meet Christ at my death. And should he return and gather the nations before him to separate the sheep from the goats, I want to be ready for that too.

Christ's Three Commandments at the Last Supper

On Thursday, Jesus sent two of his disciples to prepare the Passover meal. That night, after sunset, Jesus and his disciples joined them to share this special meal.[3] Jesus knew, as he sat with his disciples that evening, that before the night was out, he would be arrested and the next morning, he would be tried, stripped, beaten, and then tortured to death on a cross.

The Last Supper comprises 11 verses of Matthew, 10 verses of Mark, and 25 verses in Luke. But it comprises five full chapters, 155 verses, in John. When Christians commemorate the Last Supper during Holy Week, we call it Maundy Thursday. Maundy comes from the Latin word, *mandatum,* which means command. At the Last Supper, Jesus gave three commands or mandates to his disciples, and to us: Love one another, serve one another, and remember me.

Love One Another (John 13:34-35)

In John 13:34-35, Jesus said to his disciples, "I give you a new commandment: Love each other. Just as I have loved you, so you also must love each other. This is how everyone will know that you are my disciples, when you love each other" (John 13:34-35). In John 15:12-13 he resumes this teaching, saying, "This is my commandment: love each other just as I have loved you. No one has greater love than to give up one's life for one's friends." And then he says this once more in John 15:17, "I give you these commandments so that you can love each other."

We are to love our neighbor, to love our enemies, and to love one another. *This is the defining mark of the Christian life.*

As we have learned, the central focus of Jesus's teaching and preaching is the kingdom of God, and the *central ethical command* of his teaching is the call to love (*agape*). We are to love our neighbor, to love our enemies, and to love one another. *This is the defining mark of the Christian life.* It is not a feeling, but a way of living and being. It is reflected in kindness, generosity, compassion, and forgiveness. It is meant to be the currency of the kingdom of God. I've often described *agape* as a dogged determination to seek the best for the other, to bless, to build up, to care for the other.

First John 4 notes,

> *We love because God first loved us. Those who say, "I love God" and hate their brothers or sisters are liars. After all, those who don't love their brothers or sisters whom they have seen can hardly love God whom they have not seen! This commandment we have from him: Those who claim to love God ought to love their brother and sister also.*
>
> *(1 John 4:19-21)*

This call to love, to practice *agape*, is clearly given in all four Gospels and all of the New Testament epistles.[4]

It cannot be overstated that the central ethic of Jesus, powerfully captured in his own death on the cross, is the call to love. If you don't get this, you've missed the message of Christ altogether. Sadly today, Christianity is often associated with everything but love.

My youngest daughter, Rebecca, and I were having a late-night conversation recently. She said, "Dad, so often the Christians I see hardly seem loving. I watch their comments on social media, condemning other people. I see them in the news, championing political causes that hardly seem compassionate. I watch the political candidates they support who are bullies and mean-spirited. Why in the world would anyone who wasn't a Christian want to become *that* today?"

I asked her if that was the kind of Christianity she saw in her mom and me (though we are far from perfect). She said, "No, you guys aren't that way." "What about the Christians you know from our church?" "No, they are not that way." I asked about her friends who were Christians, and she agreed they reflected love not judgment or a mean spirit. I said, "I think the vast majority of Christians seek to love. Most understand that to follow Jesus is to practice love. The challenge is that often the most vocal Christians seem also to be the least loving; some of them seem more interested in using Jesus to further their causes, than in Jesus using them to further his causes."

At the Last Supper, Jesus said to his disciples "This is how everyone will know that you are my disciples, when you love each other" (John 13:35).

Serve One Another (Luke 22:25-26)

Let's turn to a second world-changing set of words Jesus spoke at the Last Supper, as recorded in Luke. His disciples, still not grasping what was about to happen to Jesus, and the kind of kingdom he was ushering in, were debating about which of them was "the greatest." Imagine arguing about that at the Last Supper. Jesus intervened saying, "The kings of the Gentiles rule over their subjects, and those in authority over them are called 'friends of the people.' But that's not the way it will be with you. Instead, the greatest among you must become like a person of lower status and the leader like a servant" (Luke 22:25-26).

John makes the same point by showing Jesus taking the role of a household servant and washing his disciples' feet at the Last Supper. After he had done so he said to them, "If I, your Lord and teacher, have washed your feet, you too must wash each other's feet. I have given you an example: Just as I have done, you also must do" (John 13:14-15).

In Matthew and Mark this conversation happens in a different setting. In Mark 10:43-45, for example, James and John came to Jesus asking that he choose them to be his top leaders when he announced himself as the Messiah. When the other disciples learned of this, they were understandably irritated. Then Jesus said to all the disciples, "Whoever wishes to become great among you must be your servant, and whoever wishes to be first among you must be slave of all. *For the Son of Man came not to be served but to serve, and to give his life a ransom for many*" (Mark 10:43-45 NRSV).

I was thinking recently about a man whose heart and life were changed, who experienced real repentance, and who came to live what Jesus taught in these first two mandates at the Last Supper. This man's name was Oskar Schindler. You may remember his story from the 1993 film, *Schindler's List*. In his early adulthood, Schindler was something of a playboy and an opportunistic German living in Poland. He was Catholic and a Nazi and failed to see that these were incompatible. He acquired a factory in Krakow and used his Nazi connections to allow him to use Jewish slave laborers from the prison camps to enrich himself.

But over time, Schindler began to see the humanity of his Jewish workers and the gross inhumanity of the Nazis. He began bribing the Nazi officials to protect his workers and their families. In 1944, the SS was closing prison camps in Krakow and preparing to ship the prisoners to Auschwitz and other camps where they would be murdered or die in the horrific conditions. Oskar Schindler developed a plan to convince the

Nazis to allow him to relocate his factory and to take his Jewish slave labor force with him. He provided to the SS a list of names of Jews he "needed" for his factory, and bribed the officials in order to save those on the list.

Over 1,100 Jews[5] were spared because of his efforts. Schindler ended up broke and bankrupt, having given his fortune as "a ransom for many." He was an unlikely hero, but to this day, Jews still visit his grave, the only former Nazi buried in Jerusalem. Schindler came to paint a dramatic picture of what it means to love and serve others.

Remember Me (1 Corinthians 11:23-26)

The earliest written account of the events of the Last Supper, and Jesus's words at it, comes not from the Gospels, but from Paul's first letter to the Corinthians. The earliest Gospel, Mark, was likely written in the mid- to late-sixties or the early seventies. Paul wrote 1 Corinthians in the early- to mid-fifties. In 1 Corinthians 11:23-26, Paul records Jesus's words at the Last Supper,

> *I received a tradition from the Lord, which I also handed on to you: on the night on which he was betrayed, the Lord Jesus took bread. After giving thanks, he broke it and said, "This is my body, which is for you; do this to remember me." He did the same thing with the cup, after they had eaten, saying, "This cup is the new covenant in my blood. Every time you drink it, do this to remember me." Every time you eat this bread and drink this cup, you broadcast the death of the Lord until he comes.*

Bread and wine were common at supper in the first century world. Wine was safer to drink than water, and bread was a staple at every meal. At this meal Jesus transformed the meaning of the Passover. The Passover was an annual remembrance and retelling of the events surrounding God's deliverance of his people from slavery in Egypt. Henceforth, for Jesus's disciples, this meal would be about Jesus's suffering and death by which he rescues us from slavery to sin and death.

As we learned in chapter 4, they saw this meal as an opportunity not only to remember Jesus but also to receive him as they shared in this holy meal.

In the early church, as Jesus's followers gathered together, they would share in a meal of bread and wine and remember and receive him. Over time that meal became the sacrament of Holy Communion. But I wonder if Jesus might have had something else in mind.

As noted above, bread and wine were a staple at most meals in the ancient world. I wonder if Jesus may have intended that at *every meal* we might pause and remember him. Our mealtime grace is a moment to remember him, and to invite him once again to be the bread of life for us. At every meal, I give thanks, and I invite Christ to fill me, form me, and feed me with the bread that gives eternal life.

Love one another, serve one another, and remember Jesus. These were the three mandates, the three final commands he gave that first Maundy Thursday, commands we're meant to live each day.

Words from Gethsemane

That night, after supper, Jesus led his disciples to a place on the Mount of Olives, across the Kidron Valley from Jerusalem, a place John tells us was a garden. Mark and Matthew call it Gethsemane (a word that means "olive press"). Luke simply tells us it was the Mount of Olives. Here's Luke's account,

> *Jesus left and made his way to the Mount of Olives, as was his custom, and the disciples followed him. When he arrived, he said to them, "Pray that you won't give in to temptation." He withdrew from them about a stone's throw, knelt down, and prayed. He said, "Father, if it's your will, take this cup of suffering away from me. However, not my will but your will must be done."*
>
> *(Luke 22:39-42)*

Perhaps the most powerful place I've prayed when visiting Jerusalem is the Basilica of Christ's Agony, or as it is more commonly known, the Church of All Nations. Sitting just above the Kidron Valley, at the base of the Mount of Olives, it is the traditional location of the garden of Gethsemane. Just outside the church is a grove of very old olive trees. Stepping inside the church, the art and architecture are meant to transport the worshipper back to that night when Christ was agonizing in the garden, as his disciples fell asleep, and to the moment when Judas betrayed Jesus with a kiss, and the soldiers arrested Jesus.

There has been a church on this location since the 300s. Evidence of a ritual bath from the first century was recently found. The current church was opened in 1924, funded by donations from Catholics from twelve countries, hence the name Church of All Nations.

Basilica of Christ's Agony (Church of All Nations) in Jerusalem

Upon entering one notices how dim it is. You are meant to feel that you are present that dreadful night. The arches above the columns are decorated in tile mosaics as tree branches that expand overhead. The domes supported by the arches are adorned with stars in the sky.

Looking to the front of the church, there are three large tile mosaics. In the center, the apse portrays Christ, resting against a rock, praying in agony. To the left of the apse, there is Judas betraying Jesus with a kiss. I have stood there many times contemplating the moments when I have betrayed Jesus. Jesus said to Judas, "Judas, would you betray the Human One with a kiss?" (Luke 22:48). Judas betrayed Jesus for thirty pieces of silver—a month's wages. I have done so for much less.

To the right of the apse, another mosaic with a crowd. There are the soldiers who have fallen back in response to Jesus's words, "I Am." This is John's account of the event. The mosaic

Images of the tile mosaics at the Basilica of Christ's Agony (Church of All Nations). Top left: Judas betraying Jesus with a kiss. Top right: John's account of the soldiers falling back in response to Jesus's proclamation of "I Am." Bottom left: Christ resting against a rock, praying in agony.

includes John's description of Peter, with his small sword, having just lopped off the ear of Malchus, the servant of the high priest.

Matthew tells us Jesus responded to the attack upon the servant by saying, "Put the sword back into its place. All those who use the sword will die by the sword" (Matthew 26:52). Luke the physician tells us that Jesus, in an act of compassion, healed the servant's ear (Luke 22:51).

In front of the altar there is an exposed rock formation, undoubtedly left exposed in the earlier fourth and twelfth century churches as well. At one time it was much higher, but I'm told that visitors used to bring their chisels and take home pieces of it to remember Christ's agony.

People kneeling in prayer around the exposed rock formation in front of the altar at the Basilica of Christ's Agony (Church of All Nations)

There is room on three sides of the stone formation for persons to kneel and actually touch the rock as they pray. There is something very powerful about this experience; it makes it somehow more real, anchoring the story in a real place. Each time I have knelt to pray, I've reflected first on Christ's agony and his anxiety in that moment. Matthew says that Jesus "began to be grieved and agitated" (Matthew 26:37 NRSV). The CEB has, "he began to feel sad and anxious." Matthew's account continues, "Then he said to them, 'I am deeply grieved, even to death; remain here, and stay awake with me.' And going a little farther, he threw himself on the ground" (Matthew 26:38-39a NRSV).

It was then that he prayed, "My Father, if it is possible, may this cup be taken from me. Yet not as I will, but as you will" (Matthew 26:39b NIV). As I kneel at the rock formation, I join him in this prayer, "Father, not my will, but thy will be done."

The Trials

Shortly after, Jesus was arrested, and his disciples fled. Jesus was taken for trial before the Jewish ruling council. That night they brought witnesses to testify against him in what was a kangaroo court. Matthew tells us, "Jesus was silent" (Matthew 26:63). When the high priest finally asked, "Are you the Christ, the Son of the blessed one?" (Mark 14:61). Jesus spoke up and said, "I am. And you will see the Human One sitting on the right side of the Almighty and coming on the heavenly clouds" (Mark 14:62). This is the second time in the Synoptics when Jesus may have used *ego eimi* in some sense to identify himself with God (or it may simply have been a response to the question. Are you? I am). Jesus then quotes Daniel 7:13 about the human one coming on clouds of heaven. By the time of Jesus these words were associated with the Messiah. Daniel 7:14 goes on to say,

> *Rule, glory, and kingship were given to him;*
> *all peoples, nations, and languages will serve him.*
> *His rule is an everlasting one—*
> *it will never pass away!—*
> *his kingship is indestructible."*

The response of the high priest and ruling council to Jesus's words and citation of Daniel 7:13 was swift.

> *Then the high priest tore his clothes and said, "Why do we need any more witnesses? You've heard his insult against God. What do you think?"*

They all condemned him. "He deserves to die!"

Some began to spit on him. Some covered his face and hit him.
(Mark 14:63-65a)

The next morning, they took him to Pontius Pilate, demanding that he be put to death. The accusation? That Jesus was claiming to be the king of the Jews

Pilate asks Jesus, "Are you the king of the Jews?" In Mark's Gospel, Jesus's response is cryptic, "That's what you say." Pilate asked him again saying, " 'Aren't you going to answer? What about all these accusations?' But Jesus gave no more answers, so that Pilate marveled" (Mark 15:2-5). Pilate then asked the crowd what he should do with Jesus, and they responded, "Crucify him!" (v. 13). And that is what Pilate did.[6]

The Seven Last Words from the Cross

According to Mark 15:25, It was nine o'clock in the morning when they crucified him. Luke 23:44 says it was 3 p.m. ("the ninth hour") when Jesus died. For six hours, Jesus hung on the cross, slowly dying.[7] It was during this time, the Gospels record, Jesus spoke the "seven last words"—not actually words, but statements. These were literally Jesus's dying words. Matthew and Mark share the same words, just one phrase. Luke has three different statements, and John has three as well, different from any in Matthew, Mark, or Luke.

A brief word about crucifixion. The process seemed aimed at three things. 1. Public humiliation of the victims; victims were crucified naked, their crime was on a sign above their head, and they were crucified, if possible, where MANY could see them. 2. To strike fear in the hearts of all observers so that it would serve as a deterrent against committing similar crimes. And 3. To maximize both the intensity and duration of pain for the victim.

Victims of crucifixion might survive on the cross into the second day, perhaps longer. There has been great debate about the actual cause of death—asphyxiation, congestive heart failure, blood clots, blood loss, and more. Whatever the final cause, it seems likely that in order to speak, one had to pull oneself up by the nails in the wrist. To do that brought great pain. This may be why, though Jesus hung on the cross for six hours, we have only seven statements from those hours of agony. If it inflicted pain for Jesus to speak, then every word must be counted as important.[8]

It is common on Good Friday, the day Christ was crucified, for Christians to recall these words and meditate upon them, whether in special services, often called "Tenebrae" services, or privately. Every Good Friday I recite these words of Jesus between 9:00 and 3:00 p.m., meditate upon their meaning, and pray about them. I find it to be a deeply meaningful practice. Here, I will only offer a few thoughts on each of these.[9]

1. "Here is your Son . . . Here is your mother." (John 19:26-27)

Only John tells us that Jesus's mother was standing near the cross, along with the disciple John. In his agony, Jesus pulls himself up by his wrists in order to demonstrate his concern for his mother. He entrusts her care to his closest disciple. To his mother he says, nodding toward John, "Here is your son." And to John he says, "Here is your mother." When I ponder these words, I am convicted by them and wonder how I might more fully care for my own mother.

2. "Father, forgive them, for they don't know what they're doing." (Luke 23:34)

Jesus regularly forgave sinners. He taught his disciples to forgive. He taught them to pray, "Forgive us our debts, as we forgive our debtors" (Matthew 6:12). He told them to love their enemies, to pray for those who wronged them, to turn the other check, and to be merciful. The Greek word for forgive is *aphiemi,* which means to release or let go.

I find it easy to forgive some people. But the deeper the pain, the harder and longer it takes me to forgive. Jesus didn't have days or weeks or months to forgive. He had six hours as he hung on the cross. Those who condemned him and sought to humiliate him were standing nearby, continuing to their hurl their insults.

Often forgiveness is something we extend to release ourselves from bitterness and resentment. Perhaps Jesus's prayer, spoken loud enough for his tormentors to hear, was a way for him to release the hate he so easily could have felt. He refused to die with hate in his heart.

Or perhaps he hoped his words, extending forgiveness, would have an impact upon his hearers. Can you imagine being part of the crowd that was cheering at his crucifixion, hearing his prayer? Did it silence their insults, if even for a moment?

But perhaps more powerful to me is the idea that, in praying this prayer from the cross, Jesus was asking for forgiveness not only for those standing at the cross, but for all of humanity, including you and me. As he offered his life to God, he did so saying, "Father, forgive them." He was giving himself as a "ransom for many." In this prayer we see an act of atonement as Jesus offered himself to his Father, as if to say, "I give myself for their sins, and ask you, Father, to forgive these small-minded humans who cannot see how hopelessly lost they are. Forgive them."

3. "Today you will be with me in paradise" (Luke 23:43)

Luke calls the criminals crucified on either side of Jesus *kakourgon*—"doers of evil." They were convicted criminals themselves, yet from their crosses, they hurled insults at Jesus. Interestingly, even as they were dying by crucifixion, they still longed to find someone they could feel superior to. But after hearing Jesus pray for God's forgiveness for his tormentors, one of the thieves spoke up for Jesus. Then he turned to Jesus and said, "Jesus, remember me when you come into your kingdom" (Luke 23:42).

Jesus replied to the criminal on the cross, "I assure you that today you will be with me in paradise." I love so many things about these words. They show that to the very end, Jesus was trying to "seek and save the lost" (Luke 19:10). Despite his pain and suffering, he's still offering grace to people who've made terrible decisions and done bad things. If Jesus offered such grace to the criminal on the cross, will he not also forgive you and me? Notice that Jesus's forgiveness did not eliminate the judicial consequences of the man's actions, but it did promise the man he would be among the righteous dead after death. (We'll speak more about this conversation in chapter 6.)

If Jesus offered such grace to the criminal on the cross, will he not also forgive you and me?

4. "I am thirsty." (John 19:28)

John tells us Jesus says, "I am thirsty." What an odd thing to record. Except that in John nearly everything has a deeper meaning. On the one hand, Jesus was likely thirsty, as often happens when people are dying. On many occasions I've fed ice chips, or held up a cup with a straw, to the lips of someone who was dying.

But for the deeper meaning, remember that in John's Gospel, Jesus offered living water to a Samaritan woman at the well (John 4:1-42). In John 7:37-38 he said, "Let anyone who is thirsty come to me and drink. Whoever believes in me, as Scripture has said, rivers of living water will flow from within them" (NIV). I believe John wants us to feel the agony and to experience with pathos the fact that the one who was the source of living water, was himself thirsty as he died, as if the living water had run dry.

5. My God, my God, why have you forsaken me?" (Mark 15:34)

After six hours hanging on the cross, Jesus cries out these words, "My God, my God, why have you forsaken me?" (NRSV). This is sometimes called the cry of dereliction because in the prayer Jesus appears to be saying that God had abandoned him—that his Father is derelict in his duties.

These words were first uttered, or penned, by King David in Psalm 22:1-2. Here's the full quote,

> *My God, my God, why have you forsaken me?*
> *Why are you so far from helping me, from the words*
> *of my groaning?*
> *O my God, I cry by day, but you do not answer;*
> *and by night, but find no rest. (NRSV)*

In 2023, after a school shooting at Covenant School in Nashville, I saw a photo of a woman standing nearby, grief on her face. She held up a sign that simply read, "Why? Why?" This was the very word Jesus spoke from the cross, "Why?" So many times, I've reminded people of Jesus's words from the cross when they are struggling with doubt, or angry with God. There are many people who have abandoned their faith in the midst of these times, or as a result of them.

But the very act of crying out this prayer is an act of faith. As we will see in the next prayer, also from the Psalms, Jesus had not abandoned all faith in God. He chose to still have hope.

6. "Father, into your hands I commit my spirit." (Luke 23:46)

Of Jesus's seven last statements from the cross, three were prayers, and two of those three are psalms. In this case it is Psalm 31:5. "Father, into your hands I commit my spirit" (NIV). Clearly Jesus prayed the Scriptures, taking texts and using them to shape his own prayers.

Twentieth-century Scottish pastor and scholar William Barclay notes in his commentary on Luke that this verse from the Psalms was one Jewish mothers taught their children to pray at bedtime, a bit like mothers used to teach their children, "Now I lay me down to sleep, and pray the Lord my soul to keep." How tender to imagine that as he was dying, with his mother standing nearby, Jesus prayed aloud the prayer she had taught him as a small boy.

Despite just crying out, "My God, my God, why have you forsaken me," Jesus's final prayer from the cross is a prayer of trust. It is one we can pray, even when we are afraid, or feeling alone or abandoned, or wrestling with doubt: "Father, into your hands I commit my spirit."

Like Jesus, this is a prayer that we might pray at bedtime each night, but also at times when we're afraid or in pain, "Father, into your hands I commit my spirit."

7. "It is finished." (John 19:30)

Jesus's final words, "It is finished" (NRSV), were actually, in Greek, just one word, *tetelestai*. It comes from a word that means completed, fulfilled, accomplished, or reaching a goal. I used to read these words as a cry of defeat. But I came to see they were a shout of victory. Bishop Will Willimon noted this word might be the kind of thing that Michelangelo could have shouted when he completed the ceiling of the Sistine Chapel.

Rightly understand, "It is finished!" makes clear that Jesus saw his death as purposeful, redemptive, and accomplishing God's saving work in order to heal a broken world. His death was an indictment on human brokenness and sin, but also a portrait of divine love and grace. And that just scratches the surface of what Christ's death accomplished.

John's Gospel begins, "In the beginning..." harkening back to the Bible's opening words in Genesis 1:1. In the Creation story, humans turned away from God. Adam and Eve essentially prayed, "Not *thy* will, but OUR will be done." A curse was unleashed, pain and hardship, sin and death had come with disobedience and rebellion. But now, a second Adam has come, and in this divine drama John sees unfolding, this Adam bore the curse for humanity, in order to heal this world. Christ's work on the cross is finished. Our work has just begun.

Chapter 6

The Resurrection and the Life

Chapter 6

The Resurrection and the Life

That [Easter] evening, while the disciples were behind closed doors because they were afraid of the Jewish authorities, Jesus came and stood among them. He said, "Peace be with you." After he said this, he showed them his hands and his side. When the disciples saw the Lord, they were filled with joy. Jesus said to them again, "Peace be with you. As the Father sent me, so I am sending you."

—John 20:19-21

"Resurrection means that the worst thing is never the last thing."
—Frederick Buechner

The Tuesday after Easter, my day began with a pastoral call expressing care for a woman whose mother died over the weekend. She watched helplessly as the paramedics tried to save her mom. Now we were discussing funeral plans. I then went to our chapel to pray with a family before the service began celebrating the life of their loved one. An hour later I was at the home of two of our members whose son had been murdered over the weekend. When I got back to the office, I learned of the passing of one of our elderly saints. I called the man's son to convey my condolences. I ended the day on my knees praying for a teenager in our congregation who lay in a coma in the hospital, the result of an automobile accident, uncertain if she would live or die.

This was not a typical day, but the concentration of tragedies and deaths left me yearning to take up the subject of this chapter, Jesus's words about death and resurrection, and the words he spoke on Easter and the days after that.

Jesus Predicts His Death… and Resurrection

Repeatedly during his ministry, Jesus told his disciples he was going to be killed. They did not understand, or if they did, they could not believe it. In Mark 8:31, Jesus said to them, "The Human One must suffer many things and be rejected by the elders, chief priests, and the legal experts, and be killed." Peter was so unsettled by Jesus's words that Mark records, "Peter took hold of Jesus and, scolding him, began to correct him" (see Mark 8:32). As you can imagine, that did not go well for Peter.

The second time Jesus predicted his death and resurrection in Mark, Mark records, "They did not understand what he was saying and were afraid to ask him" (Mark 9:32 NRSV). But it is important to note that nearly every time Jesus predicted his death in the Synoptic Gospels, he also told his disciples that *he would rise from the dead.*

I find the disciples' failure to understand Jesus's prediction of his death and resurrection, and the outright disbelief on that first Easter when the women came telling them, "Jesus is risen!" comforting for anyone who struggles with believing in the Resurrection today. When someone says, "I struggle to believe that Jesus rose from the dead," my answer is, "You are in good company. So did the disciples, and they were there!"

We'll start this chapter with some of the things Jesus said about heaven and the afterlife, then turn to his words on Easter, and finally his final words before ascending to heaven.

Jesus's Words about Heaven and the Afterlife

To listen to some Christians, you might think that the primary focus of Jesus's entire message and ministry was about heaven and how to get there. And when they speak of heaven, they mean a place where those who have accepted Christ as their Savior will dwell after they die.

The words *heaven* or *heavens* appear 130 times in the Gospels in the New Revised Standard Version (NRSV). The Greek word translated heaven is *ouranos* and its variants. This word can mean heaven or air or sky or atmosphere or the location of the stars we see at night. It can also refer to the dwelling place of God. But it often refers less to a place, and more to a reality. In Matthew, the kingdom of heaven (or the heavens as it usually is in Greek) is usually synonymous with the kingdom of God, which, as we learned in chapter 1, signifies God's reign and realm in our hearts, on earth, and throughout the cosmos.

With that in mind, let's explore some of the things Jesus says about the afterlife.

Marriage in Heaven?

As we learned in the last chapter, the last few days before he was crucified, Jesus taught in the Temple courts. Religious elites came to him with questions in the hopes of discrediting him. One of these questions had to do with the afterlife.

> *Sadducees, who deny that there is a resurrection, came to Jesus. They asked, "Teacher, Moses said,* If a man who doesn't have children dies, his brother must marry his wife and produce children for his brother. *Now there were seven brothers among us. The first one married, then died. Because he had no children he left his widow to his brother. The same thing happened with the second brother and the third, and in fact with all seven brothers. Finally, the woman died. At the resurrection, which of the seven brothers will be her husband? They were all married to her."*
>
> *Jesus responded, "You are wrong because you don't know either the scriptures or God's power. At the resurrection people won't marry nor will they be given in marriage. Instead, they will be like angels from God.*
>
> *(Matthew 22:23-30)*

Jesus avoids their trap, clarifies that he believes in the resurrection of the dead, and then notes that in the resurrection there is no more marriage. There is something in his response that bothers any who dearly love their mate. As I write this, LaVon and I are celebrating our forty-second wedding anniversary (we married the week after high school graduation). I love her so dearly. Is Jesus saying we will not still have a deep love for one another in heaven?

> **Perhaps the way we feel about close family members and our dearest friends is a picture of what love looks like in heaven.**

I don't think this is what Jesus intended, though I can't be sure. I wonder, instead, if he is telling us that in heaven there is no procreation, therefore our bodies in the afterlife will not be made for sex, and that our romantic affections and our sex drives will give way to deep friendships and the capacity to selflessly love all people in nonsexual and nonromantic ways, while still retaining a special love and relationship with those dearest to us.

The Parable of the Rich Man and Lazarus

In Luke 16, Jesus tells a parable intended to teach about the importance of showing compassion and mercy for those in need, and God's care and concern for the suffering and lowly. In a sense the parable illustrates the Beatitudes in the Sermon on the Mount and shares a common ethic with the parable of the good Samaritan and the parable of the sheep and the goats. But the parable also points to first-century Jewish conceptions of the afterlife.

Jesus said,

> *There was a certain rich man who clothed himself in purple and fine linen, and who feasted luxuriously every day. At his gate lay a certain poor man named Lazarus who was covered with sores. Lazarus longed to eat the crumbs that fell from the rich man's table. Instead, dogs would come and lick his sores.*
>
> *The poor man died and was carried by angels to Abraham's side. The rich man also died and was buried. While being tormented in the place of the dead, he looked up and saw Abraham at a distance with Lazarus at his side.*
>
> *(Luke 16:19-23)*

In the parable, the rich man begs for mercy from Abraham, asking him to allow Lazarus to provide him some relief with water. Abraham tells him,

> *Child, remember that during your lifetime you received good things, whereas Lazarus received terrible things. Now Lazarus is being comforted and you are in great pain. Moreover, a great crevasse has been fixed between us and you. Those who wish to cross over from here to you cannot. Neither can anyone cross from there to us.*
>
> *(Luke 16:25-26)*

The point of the parable is not to give a theology of heaven and hell, or even a theology of salvation; but it does offer a general picture of what happens after death that was common in first-century Judaism (and held by many Greeks as well).

Notice that the fictional Lazarus was welcomed into a blessed state Jews called, "Paradise," here represented by the bosom of Abraham. We know nothing of his life or his faith, only that he suffered during life, and God, in his mercy and compassion, ensured that in the next life, he received blessings.

On the other hand, we know the fictional rich man in the parable, despite whatever faith he would have claimed, is consigned to the place of torment, a place Jews referred to as Gehenna, because he failed to show mercy and compassion to the poor and suffering Lazarus.

The similarity to the parable of the sheep and the goats is that in that parable, the Son of Man says to the righteous, "Come, you who will receive good things from my Father. Inherit the kingdom that was prepared for you before the world began" (Matthew 25:34). The reason these were invited to receive good things was that in this life they showed mercy to the hungry, thirsty, and naked and were those who welcomed strangers and cared for the sick and imprisoned. Likewise, those who are sent away, kept from the blessed life are those who, like the rich man in the parable above, failed to show compassion and mercy to those in need.

"Today You Will Be with Me in Paradise"

In the last chapter, we touched on Jesus's words from the cross, among which are his words to a thief crucified next to him, "Today you will be with me in paradise." Let's return to those words now, for they point toward something important about Jesus's understanding of the afterlife.

As we've learned, the thief was a "doer of evil," perhaps a violent criminal. Yet as he hangs on the cross next to Jesus, he is moved to say to him, "Jesus, remember me when you come into your kingdom" (Luke 23:42). It is hard to know precisely what this man's words reflected. It is possible they simply expressed an admiration for Jesus, or perhaps a compassion for this crucified king who refused to hate his tormentors. Maybe he had faith that Jesus really was the Messiah.

Whatever the thief's motives, level of faith, or understanding of Jesus's true identity, it was enough for Jesus to respond to him, "Today, you will be with me in paradise" (Luke 23:43). Clearly this thief is not granted paradise due to his good works. Nor does he receive it because of his right theology. The thief did not know the creeds. He did not say the "sinner's prayer." He was never baptized. But he has some small measure of faith, and that was enough for Jesus to offer him mercy and to promise a welcome, that day at his death, into paradise.

I love that this man was shown mercy, despite his past. It points to the mercy and grace we see in Jesus's ministry and helps us see the heart and character of God that Jesus reveals. This gives me hope for those who, in this life, struggled. A young woman I've known her entire life recently died from a fentanyl overdose. I had baptized her when she was a little girl, gave to her a Bible in the third grade, and later confirmed her. She was a sweet young woman. But when she began experimenting with drugs as a teenager, she soon became enslaved and struggled to break free.

She'd made some bad choices, but inside, there was still just a girl who wanted to be loved by others and by God. One of the last times I'd seen her was at the county jail. While there, she asked me, "Do you think Jesus still loves me after all I've done?" The fact that she was still asking the question told me something about her heart. Jesus's words and actions toward the criminal on the cross point to the answer for this young woman, "Yes, Jesus still loves you."

At her funeral service I shared a clip from the end of the first episode of the hit television show, *The Chosen*. *The Chosen* tells the Gospel stories about Jesus but takes some liberty in developing the characters as the writers imagine them. The very first episode was focused on Mary Magdalene, though it introduced other Gospel characters as well. In this episode the writers imagined that Mary's father had died when she was a little girl and that she had grown up struggling, and eventually selling her body to men to support herself. She ends up wrestling demons, perhaps of mental illness. She self-medicates with alcohol.

Jesus is not seen until the end of the episode. Mary is drinking in a tavern where Jesus comes to find her. He tries speaking to her and she runs away. He follows and calls her by name. Then he speaks the words of Isaiah 43:1 to her, "Don't fear, for I have redeemed you; / I have called you by name; *you are mine*" (emphasis added). Jesus embraces her and she is healed in his embrace.

I wept each time I watched this final scene because it is precisely how I pictured Jesus responding to this young woman,

Holly, at her death. I pictured Jesus calling her name. I loved the idea of him speaking the words of Isaiah 43:1, and I could see Jesus holding her in his arms and healing her.

My point, as I concluded the homily at this young woman's memorial service, was that this young woman, who was loved by her parents, her daughters, and the rest of her family, was also loved by the same Jesus who welcomed Mary Magdalene and who said to the thief on the cross, "Today you will be with me in paradise."

Jesus's Words About Heaven and the Resurrection in the Gospel of John

The Synoptics offer us glimpses of heaven, but when Christians look for comfort as they approach death, their own or that of someone they love, it is usually to the Gospel of John that they turn, words we considered briefly in chapter 4.

We touched on the story of Lazarus of Bethany in chapter 4 (not the Lazarus in the parable above, but Lazarus, Jesus's friend and thee brother of Martha and Mary). John 11 records that Lazarus fell sick. Jesus did not return to Bethany in time to heal him, and so Lazarus died. This left Lazarus's sisters, Martha and Mary, deeply disappointed. When Jesus arrived in Bethany, days after Lazarus's death and burial, Martha ran to speak to Jesus.

> *Martha said to Jesus, "Lord, if you had been here, my brother wouldn't have died. Even now I know that whatever you ask God, God will give you."*

Jesus told her, "Your brother will rise again."

Martha replied, "I know that he will rise in the resurrection on the last day."

Jesus said to her, "I am the resurrection and the life. Whoever believes in me will live, even though they die. Everyone who lives and believes in me will never die."

(John 11:21-26)

Jesus's response to Martha is such a powerful and definitive word. I AM the RESURRECTION and I AM the LIFE. The United Methodist "Service of Death and Resurrection" begins with Jesus's words in this powerful I Am statement.

The story in John 11 continues,

When Mary arrived where Jesus was and saw him, she fell at his feet and said, "Lord, if you had been here, my brother wouldn't have died."

When Jesus saw her crying and the Jews who had come with her crying also, he was deeply disturbed and troubled. He asked, "Where have you laid him?

They replied, "Lord, come and see."

Jesus began to cry.

(John 11:32-35)

I love these words. Jesus knows what it is to grieve. He understands the intense sorrow we feel when we say good-bye to those we love. How grateful I am that he weeps as he sees the grief of Mary and Martha and as he contemplates Lazarus's death.

Then Jesus asks to be taken to the tomb where Lazarus's very dead body was laid four days earlier. Upon arriving he says to them, "Remove the stone." Martha, the pragmatist, says to him, "Lord, the smell will be awful! He's been dead four days." What an earthy, human statement. But Jesus persists. And when they remove the stone, "Jesus shouted with a loud voice, 'Lazarus, come out!'" (John 11:39, 43).

And then, "The dead man came out, his feet bound and his hands tied, and his face covered with a cloth. Jesus said to them, 'Untie him and let him go'" (John 11:44).

Christ knows our grief. He feels our sorrow. But he has power over our death! No wonder we read this story, or quote Jesus's words, as we bid farewell to our loved ones.

"I Go to Prepare a Place for You"

Several chapters later in John, as Jesus shares his last meal with his disciples, he tells his disciples once more that he is leaving them,

> *Don't be troubled. Trust in God. Trust also in me. My Father's house has room to spare. If that weren't the case, would I have told you that I'm going to prepare a place for you? When I go to prepare a place for you, I will return and take you to be with me so that where I am you will be too.*
>
> *(John 14:1-3)*

Don't be troubled—the Greek words involve a deep agitation of the heart. Instead, believe or trust in God and in me, Jesus says. "Trust that I'm going to prepare a place for you." In the immediate context, he is going to Calvary the next day to prepare a place for them. Jesus's death and resurrection were the climax of the Word he incarnated from God. By his suffering and death he made clear the reality of human sin, the costliness of God's grace, the depth of God's selfless and sacrificial love. The apostles heard in his suffering and death the powerful proclamation of redemption and reconciliation.

But ultimately, in his death and resurrection *and* ascension to heaven, he was preparing a place for his followers in his Father's house or family. The Greek word for house is *oikia* and it also can mean household or family—the people who live in a house.

The King James Bible, you may recall, translated Jesus's words to say that, "In my Father's house are many mansions" (John 14:2) The Greek word for mansion is *monai* and the word simply means an abode or dwelling place. I like the Common English Bible's rendering of it, "My Father's house has room to spare." I like to think of it this way, "In my Father's home, in his family, there's plenty of spare rooms and a place for you at the table and to be a part of his family. I have made sure of it!"

I am reminded that this world is not our home. Our Father's house is the home Christ has prepared for us, in his family, in a place of beauty and joy.

The Word Spoken without a Word

The focus of this book is the message of Jesus. The climax of that message is Jesus's death and resurrection. In this case, the climax of the message of Jesus was not one he spoke with his lips.

The Word made flesh, the I Am, the Good Shepherd, the Bread of Life, the Light of the World, offered his most powerful message as he hung on the cross and as he rose from the dead.

When it comes to explaining the meaning of Christ's death and how it "works," the New Testament authors rely on metaphors. They speak of it as redemption, a reflection of divine love, a ransom, reconciliation, atonement, an indictment on human sin, and more.

I believe the death of Christ is less like a judicial transaction, and more like poetry. It is a word from God about human brokenness and sin and the lengths to which God will go to heal and forgive us. It is a word about human cruelty and inhumanity and about the depth of God's love and grace. The cross is a message that some only see as foolish, but others find in it the power of God (1 Corinthians 1:18). We don't ever fully understand the cross, but we are seized by its message and transformed as we seek to follow our crucified king.

I am reminded, when I think of Jesus's death on the cross, of the story of Richard Manning and his friend Ray Brennan serving in the Marines together in Korea. A North Korean grenade was tossed into their bunker. Ray looked at the grenade, looked at his friend Richard, and then threw himself on the grenade, smothering the explosion with his body and saving his friend Richard. Richard, as you may know, came back from the war and changed his first name to Brennan as a tribute to the man who gave his life that he might live. Brennan Manning went on to have a profound influence on many people through his writings about life and faith.

When we *hear* the message of Christ's death, really hear and accept that it was for us, we find ourselves changed. And we take on his name and seek to live as his followers.

> **When we hear the message of Christ's death, really hear and accept that it was for us, we find ourselves changed.**

But the climax of Christ's message was not only his death, it was his resurrection. These cannot be separated. By raising Christ from the dead, God made clear that evil, hate, sin, and death do not have the final word. Though the darkness tried to extinguish the light, it ultimately could not overcome it. In the end, light overcomes darkness, love conquers hate, and life vanquishes death.

The apostle Paul, quoting both Hosea and Isaiah to describe the import of Jesus's resurrection, wrote, "Death has been swallowed up in victory." / "Where, O death, is your victory? / Where, O death, is your sting?" (1 Corinthians 15:54b-55 NRSV, quoting Isaiah 25:8 and Hosea 13:14). I frequently turn to the words I think were first coined by Frederick Buechner. If you've read my books you've read them before: "Easter means the worst thing is never the last thing." There is always hope.

My wife and I sat with my mother-in-law on a Monday morning. Her breathing had become more shallow. She hadn't spoken, or opened her eyes, in twenty-four hours. The hospice nurse articulated what we already knew, that she was very near the end. She opened her eyes—whether it was an autonomic response or an intentional act, I don't know. I spoke to her with gentleness and love, "There you are!" I don't know if she could see us, but imagined it was one last opportunity to see our faces as we read the words of Jesus to her, "I go to prepare a place for you . . ." Through our tears we anointed her head with oil, sang a hymn, and told her we loved her. And then she took her last breath.

The sorrow and grief were mitigated by the words of Jesus, "I am the resurrection and the life, those who believe in me will never die" and by the knowledge that she had heard his voice welcoming her home and was, as the hymn goes, united with "all the saints who from their labor rest." But it was not just the words of Jesus that give this hope; it was his own resurrection from the dead. As St. Paul noted, we grieve as people who have hope.

That leads us to the words of Jesus in the Gospels on Easter and on the days after that.

The Easter Questions of Jesus

It is interesting that the greatest teacher who ever walked the earth asked more questions than he answered. The first time we meet Jesus in the Gospels, after his infancy, is in Luke 2:46 where he's twelve years old and sitting in the Temple asking the religious leaders questions. Throughout his ministry, by some accounts, he asked 305 questions. And while he was often asked questions, he seldom directly answered. Instead he often answered with more questions.

Socrates was known for using this method of teaching. Knowing the power of people discovering the answer for themselves, he asked the right questions. Jesus does the same.

He invites people to think and to reflect and to discover the answers to their questions. Most of us would do better to ask more questions of others, and of ourselves.

Having asked so many questions before his crucifixion, it shouldn't surprise us that on Easter and the days after, he continued to ask questions, thirteen to be exact. In some cases the questions serve to heighten the tension, but in others, to invite the one being questioned to give voice to their sorrow, or to articulate their convictions about Jesus, or to lead them to faith or restoration.

On Easter morning, the first person Jesus appeared to was Mary Magdalene. John tells us Mary thought he was the gardener. As she wept at the tomb Jesus asked her, "Woman, why are you crying? Who are you looking for?" (John 20:15). To two disciples as they walked on the road to Emmaus, who were discussing the events of the previous days, Jesus appeared as a stranger and asked, "What are you talking about as you walk along?" (Luke 24:17). And as they explained their hopes that Jesus was the Messiah, yet the reality of his death, he asked them another question, "Wasn't it necessary for the Christ to suffer these things and then enter into his glory?" (Luke 24:26). That Easter night, Jesus appeared to his disciples, and they were terrified, as if they were seeing a ghost. He asked them, "Why are you startled? Why are doubts arising in your hearts?" (Luke 24:38). Then, because they still weren't convinced he wasn't a ghost, he asked, "Do you have anything to eat?" whereupon he ate a piece of baked fish, something a ghost clearly wouldn't do (Luke 24:41-43).

I'll skip a question or two, but I want to draw your attention to John 21. The disciples had returned to the Sea of Galilee and went fishing all night and caught nothing. The story parallels the story in Luke 5 when Jesus first called Simon and Andrew, James, and John. Then, too, they'd been fishing all night and caught nothing. In John 21, set some days or weeks after Easter, as the fishermen are heading back to shore, they see a stranger who'd been cooking bread and fish over a fire on the lakeshore. And he asks, "Children, have you caught anything to eat?" Then he tells them to cast the nets on the other side of the boat, as he had done in Luke 5. And suddenly their nets were filled with fish. It is then they recognize Jesus once more.

As they come to the shoreline, Jesus feeds them bread and fish. Then he turns to Simon Peter, the disciple who denied knowing Jesus three times the night he was arrested, and Jesus asks Simon three questions. "Simon son of John, do you love me more than these?" "Simon son of John, do you love me?" and one last time, "Simon son of John, do you love me?"(John 21:15-17). Each time Peter responded that he loved Jesus. The repetition of this question pained Peter.

Why does John record this embarrassing story about Peter, and the excruciating recital of these questions three times? It was not to embarrass Peter. I believe John included the scene that his readers might remember that when we have denied Jesus by our words or actions, that Christ is willing to restore us too.

Have you ever denied Jesus? I have, a thousand times, by my thoughts, words or deeds; by what I have done or what I have left undone. I read this interchange with Peter and imagine

Jesus asking me, "Adam, son of Mark, *do* you love me?" "Lord you know I love you." "Then feed my lambs." A short time later he asks again, "Adam, son of Mark, *do* you love me?" It hurts to hear it a second time, "Yes, Lord, you know I love you." "Take care of my sheep." And then, once more, "Adam, son of Mark, *do* you love me?" It's heartbreaking, but I say again, perhaps with even more conviction for having been asked now a third time, "Lord, you know everything; you know I love you." "Feed my lambs."

That leads to the final words of Jesus in the Gospels and in Acts.

As the Father Has Sent Me, So I Am Sending You

Jesus appeared to his disciples in various ways, times and places, during the ensuing forty days following Easter. The Gospels share different Resurrection stories. But they all agree that Jesus's final message to the disciples was a charge to them to be his witnesses, his representatives, to the world.

Mark's Gospel appears to have been truncated early in its transmission. His longer ending, written after the other Gospels and drawing from all of them, offers these final words: "Go into the whole world and proclaim the good news to every creature" (Mark 16:15).

In Matthew 28:18-20, we read,

> *Jesus came near and spoke to them, "I've received all authority in heaven and on earth. Therefore, go and make disciples of all nations, baptizing them in the name of the Father and of the*

Son and of the Holy Spirit, teaching them to obey everything that I've commanded you. Look, I myself will be with you every day until the end of this present age."

In Luke, Jesus tells his disciples,

He said to them, "This is what is written: the Christ will suffer and rise from the dead on the third day, and a change of heart and life for the forgiveness of sins must be preached in his name to all nations, beginning from Jerusalem. You are witnesses of these things."

(Luke 24:46-48)

Later, in Acts, Luke would record that Jesus commanded the disciples to remain in Jerusalem, awaiting the gift of the Holy Spirit. And then he said, "You will receive power when the Holy Spirit has come upon you, and you will be my witnesses in Jerusalem, in all Judea and Samaria, and to the end of the earth" (Acts 1:8).

And finally, in John, we read, "As the Father sent me, so I am sending you." Then he breathed on them and said, "Receive the Holy Spirit. If you forgive anyone's sins, they are forgiven; if you don't forgive them, they aren't forgiven" (John 20:21-23).

The accounts of these final words and Jesus's commission differ in detail. Matthew's Great Commission happens in the Galilee. Luke's in Jerusalem. In John, Jesus gives the Holy Spirit and commissions his disciples on Easter evening. In Luke/Acts it happens some forty days after Easter, just a week before the Day of Pentecost. But in each account Jesus calls his disciples to be his witnesses, and that ultimately involves not merely telling others, but also living the message he taught them.

The Gospel writers wrote their closing words, their commission from Jesus, decades after he spoke the words to the first disciples. Most of those first disciples had died by the time the Gospels were written. Matthew, Mark, Luke, and John recorded these words not for the first disciples, but *for every generation that would come after them, including you and me.*

Which leads me to ask you a question: Having studied the message of Jesus, how will you respond to it? And how will you pass it on? I want to encourage you, before you put this book on the shelf, hand it off to a friend, or set it aside for a rummage sale, to go back through each chapter and ask, "What is Jesus asking of me?" And then to invite the Holy Spirit to fill you, guide you, and empower you, so that you, too, can answer Christ's call to be his witness in your daily life.

Having studied the message of Jesus, how will you respond to it? And how will you pass it on?

I think of my own journey to Christ. My grandmother Sarah, a devout Catholic, was instrumental in my baptism as an infant. She also taught me to pray, took me to Mass, and told me about Christ. She died when I was thirteen, but her witness shaped the rest of my life.

My Aunt Celia Belle and Uncle Dan were faithful members of the Church of Christ in Blackwell, Oklahoma.

They reflected the love of Christ to me and ensured I was in church when I visited their home. My parents took me and my sister to a United Methodist church when we were children, which planted the seeds for my one day becoming a United Methodist pastor. When I was fourteen a man named Harold Thorson knocked on my door. At the time I had rejected God and was experimenting with drugs and alcohol. Harold invited me to visit the church he attended, which I did with my mother the next weekend. There, the pastor, Phil Hollis, and the youth pastor, Gary Patterson, and a host of others so welcomed, loved me, and encouraged me that I eventually decided to follow Jesus.

I wonder who those witnesses were for you? And who will point to you as being instrumental in their coming to faith?

Each morning I wake up, slip to my knees, and pledge my life to Christ once more, and I invite the Holy Spirit to fill me, guide me, and lead me, that I, too, might be Christ's witness, sharing and living the gospel he preached. And as I do, I find my greatest joy.

Christ is calling you, each day, to bear witness to the good news he proclaimed. I invite you to say to him, "Here I am Lord, send me."

In this book, I've attempted to summarize the major themes of Jesus's message and to help you understand them and their significance for your life. There's so much more that Jesus said and did that I've not covered. I'm reminded of the words with which John ends his Gospel, "Jesus did many other things as well. If all of them were recorded, I imagine the world itself wouldn't have enough room for the scrolls that would be written" (John 21:25). I want to encourage you to read the Gospels for yourself, study them, reflect upon them, and seek to live them.

As we close, I want to conclude by sharing with you, once more, the words that Jesus spoke at the conclusion of the Sermon on the Mount,

> *Everybody who hears these words of mine and puts them into practice is like a wise builder who built a house on bedrock. The rain fell, the floods came, and the wind blew and beat against that house. It didn't fall because it was firmly set on bedrock. But everybody who hears these words of mine and doesn't put them into practice will be like a fool who built a house on sand. The rain fell, the floods came, and the wind blew and beat against that house. It fell and was completely destroyed.*
>
> *(Matthew 7:24-27)*

I encourage you to build your house on the bedrock, on the message of Jesus, who offers us "the words of life."

NOTES

Introduction

1 The allusions include a reference in 1 Timothy 5:18 though not attributed to Jesus and 1 Corinthians 7:10-11. Paul also quotes words the resurrected Christ spoke to him in 2 Corinthians 12:9.

Chapter 1. The Kingdom of God Has Come Near

1 Quoted by Mark Roberts in an excellent summary of the Kingdom called, "Jesus and the Kingdom of God." The quote is from Gordon Fee, "Jesus: Early Ministry/Kingdom of God," lecture delivered at Regent College. Tape Series 2235E, Pt. 1. Copyright © Regent College, Vancouver, B.C., Canada.

Chapter 2. The World's Most Important Sermon

1 The quote is oft repeated and may come from Bradley's 1948 Memorial Day speech at Long Meadow, Massachusetts.

2 Taken from *The Message of the Sermon on the Mount (Matthew 5-7: Christian Counter-Culture)* by John R.W. Stott (Lisle, IL: InterVarsity Press, 1985), 1.

3 Lanre Dahunsi. "Kurt Vonnegut 1999 Commencement Speech at Agnes Scott College," November 4, 2020. https://www.youtube.com/watch?v=VDMfMfgNsDM see 5:42-5:52.

4 John Winthrop, "A Model of Christian Charity," in *A Library of American Literature: Early Colonial Literature, 1607-1675*, Edmund Clarence Stedman and Ellen Mackay Hutchinson, eds. (New York: 1892), 307.

5 NPR. "Rev. Kyles Remembers Martin Luther King, Jr." NPR, January 17, 2010. https://www.npr.org/templates/story/story.php?storyId=122670935.

6 Martin Luther King Jr, *Stride Toward Freedom: The Montgomery Story* (Boston: Beacon), 71.

7 "Service of Christian Marriage," *The United Methodist Hymnal* (Nashville: The United Methodist Publishing House, 1989), 867.

8 Allianz Life. "Nearly 2 in 3 Americans Worry More About Running Out of Money Than Death," n.d. accessed August 16, 2024, https://www.allianzlife.com/about/newsroom/2024-press-releases/nearly-2-in-3-americans-worry-more-about-running-out-of-money-than-death.

9 Lyle Daly, "Nearly Three-Quarters of Americans Stress About Money Monthly. Here's How to Stop," *The Motley Fool*, February 2, 2024, https://www.fool.com/the-ascent/personal-finance/articles/nearly-three-quarters-of-americans-stress-about-money-monthly-heres-how-to-stop/.

Chapter 3. He Spoke to Them in Parables

1 George A. Buttrick, *The Parables of Jesus* (Grand Rapids: Baker, 1973), 7.

2 C. H. Dodd, *The Parables of the Kingdom* (New York: McMillan, 1961), 16.

3 See my book, *Luke: Jesus and the Outsiders, Outcasts, and Outlaws* (Nashville: Abingdon, 2022).

Chapter 4. Who Do YOU Say that I Am?

1 Gail R. O'Day, "The Gospel of John," in *The New Interpreter's Bible*, Luke, John (Nashville: Abingdon Press, 1995), 9: 497–98.

2 Some scholars look at some of Jesus's metaphors in John as parables, but most scholars suggest that there is not a single parable in the Gospel of John like the kind Jesus tells in Matthew, Mark, and Luke.

3 Some say as many as two thousand.

4 In Hebrew, God's response is *'eh-yeh asher 'eh-yeh:* "I Am who I Am." But then in Exodus 3:15 God says to Moses, "Say to the Israelites, 'YHWH, (The LORD) the God of your ancestors, Abraham's God, Isaac's God, and Jacob's God, has sent me to you.' This is my name forever; this is how all generations will remember me." Which is God's name, 'Eh-yeh or YHWH? They are slightly different forms of the verb "to be" but 'Eh-yeh is not used again as God's name. Henceforth it is YHWH that will appear as God's name.

5 See my chapter on "Are All Non-Christians Going to Hell?" in *Wrestling with Doubt, Finding Faith* (Nashville: Abingdon, 2023).

Chapter 5. Final Words

1 Kettering Health, "Life's Brevity and Last Words." *Strive Newsletter*, March 18, 2022, https://ketteringhealth.org/lifes-brevity-and-last-words/.

2 For a more in-depth look at the last twenty-four hours of Jesus's life and the final words he spoke, see my books, *24 Hours That Changed the World* (Nashville: Abingdon, 2009) and *Final Words from the Cross* (Nashville: Abingdon, 2011).

3 The chronology I mention is from the Synoptic Gospels. For John, the Last Supper is on Wednesday night, at what appears to be an ordinary evening meal so that, according to his chronology, Jesus is crucified on the Preparation Day for the Passover, the day the lambs were sacrificed as seen in John 19:14-15, "It was about noon on the Preparation Day for the Passover. Pilate said to the Jewish leaders, 'Here's your king.' The Jewish leaders cried out, 'Take him away! Take him away! Crucify him!'"

4 The exception is Acts of the Apostles where it is practiced, but not named as *agape*.

5 Sources vary from 1,100 to 1,200—I used 1,100 as this is what is shown in the film.

6 I am intentionally turning to Mark, the earliest Gospel, and most abbreviated, for his account here. The other accounts are equally spartan, though there are some differences between them.

7 As noted earlier, John has Jesus crucified on the Day of Preparation for the Passover, not on the morning after the Passover began. And in John, Jesus is sentenced to die "about noon" (John 19:14) and would have been crucified sometime that afternoon. It was the afternoon of that day that the Passover lambs were sacrificed and slaughtered. John, who earlier in the Gospel refers to Jesus as the "Lamb of God," likely intends his chronology to coincide with the slaughter of the lambs on that afternoon.

8 We can't know if Jesus spoke more than these seven sayings, but the Gospels record at least these seven. Matthew and Mark only record one phrase during that entire six hours.

9 For a more in-depth study of these seven final statements of Jesus, see my book, *Final Words from the Cross* (Nashville: Abingdon, 2011).

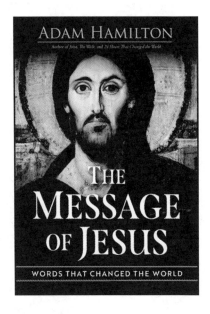